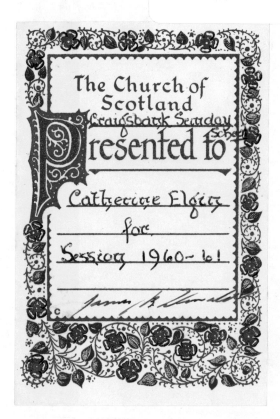

The Church of
Scotland

Craigsbank Sunday
School

Presented to

Catherine Elgin

for

Session 1960-61

James B. _____

Kathleen Ferrier

Red Lion Lives

Kathleen Ferrier

by

PETER LETHBRIDGE

RED LION LIVES

CASSELL · LONDON

CASSELL & COMPANY LTD
35 Red Lion Square . London W.C1
and at
MELBOURNE · SYDNEY · TORONTO · CAPE TOWN
JOHANNESBURG · AUCKLAND

———

© Cassell & Co. Ltd. 1959
First published 1959

Set in 11 pt. Baskerville type, and printed in Great Britain
by Wyman & Sons, Ltd., London, Fakenham and Reading
F.859

ACKNOWLEDGEMENTS

MY most grateful thanks are due to Mr. Roy Henderson for his kindness in telling me several ancedotes of Kathleen Ferrier, none of which have been published before; he has also allowed me to trespass on his time by answering innumerable questions of mine regarding Glyndebourne and many other details connected with the world of music. Above all, not only myself but the readers are in his dept for his allowing me to make extracts from the original unpublished letter quoted in Chapter XIII. It is also by his kind permission and that of the publishers, Messrs. Hamish Hamilton Ltd., that I have been able to make the two quotations from his chapter 'Per Ardua . . .' in *Kathleen Ferrier, A Memoir* edited by Neville Cardus.

Mr. Gerald Moore generously gave me much of his extremely valuable time, and besides answering so many questions with infinite patience, supplied some details of his friendship and work with Miss Ferrier. My thanks to him also for allowing me to see the room where she spent the last months of her life.

I must thank my friend Miss Winifred Cross as well for help and advice, and for reading the proofs.

P.L.

CHAPTER

1

LESS than a century ago many people in foreign lands were inclined to think of the English as being the most unmusical nation in the world. Today nothing could be further from the truth; but it is a legend that persists, in spite of famous orchestras such as the Hallé and the London Philharmonic; the Henry Wood Promenade Concerts; and the Glyndebourne Opera, which presents in the green and lovely Sussex Weald productions every bit as exquisite as anything at Salzburg or Vienna.

True, we have not the numerous small opera houses in provincial towns and cities, such as are to be met with all over Italy and France, Belgium and Germany. And every so often there is an ominous paragraph in the newspapers: 'Future of Covent Garden Opera in peril. Government subsidies must be increased, or opera in London may cease!' Luckily, of late years, such headlines have been just scares, a possibility not likely to be realized. But still Paris, Milan, Vienna and Rome raise an eyebrow; the good citizens, secure in their own opera houses, shrug their shoulders and say: 'Ah, those English—not only have they mixed up their opera with a cabbage market for two hundred years—now they're getting rid of it altogether . . . !'

It is only the English who come in for this sort of thing. All the world knows the music of Wales, and stands in respect and awe before the beauty of Welsh singing; while Scotland, from the Border Country to the misty enchantment of the Western Isles, plucks at the heart-strings with her haunting music; and just across the water—well, no one could call the Irish unmusical.

But what of England? While it is true that big concerts are restricted to London and the larger provincial cities such as Manchester, Liverpool, Bristol and Birmingham, there are, throughout the land, hundreds and thousands of people who find joy in making music—by belonging to music and choral societies (such as those in Bradford and Leeds), and numerous other gatherings, often in quite small towns and certainly in many larger villages.

This is something that has never died out since the days of the first Queen Elizabeth four hundred years ago. Then the English were known as the most musical people in Europe. No one could call his or herself in any way cultured who could not read a part at sight; who was not well versed in madrigal and ballad; and who could not, at the given moment, take up an instrument and join with others in weaving the melody of 'Greensleeves' or 'Fair House of Joy and Bliss'. If you were a young lady, you must play at least passably well on the virginals, that early version of the pianoforte; or if a young man, prove yourself expert with lute, viol, cithern or flute.

2

It so happens that every now and again, someone is born in these islands who is destined to bring lasting musical fame to themselves and their country. But it is an event rare enough for the names of these favoured ones to long outlast their own lifetime. Very often such people are born in circumstances and a setting far removed from anything to do with the musical world; and this was what happened when, in the village of Higher Walton in Lancashire, not far from Blackburn, there was born on 22nd April, 1912, Kathleen Mary Ferrier.

Kathleen was the second daughter of a musical village schoolmaster, William Ferrier, and his wife Alice. They were typical North Country folk, warm hearted and kindly, with the rather shrewd but always very human no-nonsense way of dealing with the world about them. Money had never been plentiful, but they could look at life with humour and tolerance, and if their children were not brought up in plenty, there was always enough. It was a comfortable, secure home for a little girl to be born into, and there was something more. The whole family was interested in music, and though the opportunities for anything more than amateur concerts with friends of like tastes did not come their way, the background was there. Also, between them, William and Alice Ferrier gave their children a mixture of Scots, Irish, Welsh and English blood; little dreaming that all four strains were to soar into musical prodigy in Kathleen.

There was nothing unduly strange in the Ferrier family being musical; all over the North, from Liverpool to Newcastle, from Kendal to Bradford, thousands of ordinary people take an enormous interest in making music, listening to it, and discuss and criticize it far more than in the South.

When Kathleen was about eighteen months old, her family moved from Higher Walton to Blackburn not many miles away. There she was to live for the next twenty-two years the life of an ordinary Lancashire girl, outwardly little different from thousands of others of the same environment, save for an added talent for piano playing and what must have been a growingly brilliant but completely untrained voice. The other world, that one of arduous training, and the fame that brought concert tours in Europe and America, would have seemed like the ravings of a lunatic if either Kathleen or any member of the Ferrier family had been told of what lay in the distant future. More probably they would have roared with laughter at the idea of 'Our Kath' becoming a world famous singer with a glorious voice such as has been given to few in any century, and would have told the prophet, 'Don't be daft, luv!' For though Blackburn is not 'clogs and shawl' Lancashire, they don't scorn clogs, or their smokier neighbours, and they would be the last to pretend that the Industrial North produces a genius from every small street.

Blackburn lies in the smoke-covered basin where some 1,830 feet above looms the romantic height of Pendle Hill, famous for its legends of the Lancashire Witches three hundred years ago. But if any seventeenth century Lancastrians could return today, they would recognize little of the surrounding countryside. For all this part is where the Industrial Revolution of

4

the late eighteenth and early nineteenth century struck hardest, and what the poet William Blake called 'the dark, satanic mills' send forth a day-and-night pall of black smoke to shadow the blue of heaven. You get the clearest idea of just how heavy is the perpetual haze by seeing it from many miles away. Standing on the crest of Arnside Knott, a small hill looking down the coast from the borders of Westmorland, on a clear day with all the blue and green and silver glory of the Lakeland Hills to the north, you can look southward down the coast towards industrial Lancashire, and see mile upon mile of darkened sky above the far-off mills and factories.

Yet where Lancashire has retained its countryside, no county can be more beautiful. A very short distance out of Blackburn lie the ruins of Clitheroe Castle, and there is a photograph extant of Kathleen with some friends in 1935 showing the background of scenery in Garstang, only one of the many attractive places in wild country.

Blackburn itself possesses, among classical style public buildings, a very good concert hall, and a cathedral; and the Musical Society has played an important part in the life of the town for many years. The town is ten miles from Preston, away to the west, and about twenty miles from Manchester. All around lie the cotton manufacturing towns of Bolton, Accrington, Burnley, Darwen, all with a tough, vital, population who go every Saturday in the season to cheer on their favourite football team, look forward to 'Wakes Weeks' at the end of summer, and are the fortunate owners of a sense of humour that takes them headlong through

5

life, enjoying the good times and shouldering the bad.

It was during years of war that Kathleen first lived at Blackburn—years which luckily left her untouched. Far away in France a world was shattered in flames by the guns of the Somme and Flanders; but in 1914–18 war was still fought by soldiers on battlefields. No rumble of guns reached Northern England, and Zeppelin airships mostly confined their raids to London and the eastern parts of the country. There was no need for barrage balloons or anti-aircraft gun-sites to guard the great factories and mills; that all lay ahead in another war—when the years 1939–45 were to find Kathleen going through raids in London and travelling in the acute discomfort of blacked-out, war rationed trains and hotels.

But in 1914 after William Ferrier had successfully applied for the post of head of St. Paul's School, Blackburn, it was the elder children who felt the change from country life at Walton to the more cramped living in Blackburn. Kathleen was still only a baby; and we catch no further glimpse of her until she was around three years old.

Many stories have been told of famous musicians in early childhood, who show more than normal sensitivity; a small boy given a tin violin, and breaking it violently—with a demand to be given 'a real one', a toddler listening to the piano and solemnly saying 'That's wrong' when a somewhat affronted elder strikes a wrong chord. Kathleen was no 'infant prodigy', but it seems that she liked to sound a few notes on the piano, trip away and then return—after

6

the fashion of countless other tinies. Then there came a day when, offering to pick out a tune for a cousin, Kathleen suddenly dissolved in weeping, and when asked what was the matter, expressed a fierce desire to play properly.

As befitted a schoolmaster's children, the young Ferriers were quick to learn. Kathleen learned to read even before she was sent to St. Silas' Elementary School, Blackburn, at five years old, and then not many months later to the kindergarten of the Girls' High School. Money was never plentiful, but like many other parents William and Alice Ferrier grudged no efforts for their children, and Kathleen was to remain at the more expensive school for the greater part of ten years. Her schooling was begun; and only time could tell to what career it would lead.

CHAPTER

2

A happy and contented family life is much more important to any child than plenty of money. The discontent, broken homes and restless unhappiness of our present decade, has shown this clearly to many who once thought that more money for the great majority in this country would automatically solve all problems.

Kathleen had to learn economy in clothes early, and to 'waste not want not'; but she had affectionate parents, and a close-knit family circle. And being a good mixer she easily made school-friends, some of whom remained her friends for life.

By the time the war ended in 1918, she had become good at both work and games, a fine 'all-rounder', popular both with her fellow pupils and mistresses. It is a little amusing, in view of her subsequent brilliant career, to find that some of her neighbours thought she was cut out to become a good games mistress!

Kathleen added to a bright and lovable disposition a fondness for animals, particularly cats. She liked cats for a reason all true cat lovers will recognize at once— their independence, the fact that if you once gain a cat's love it is something to be treasured. People who

8

don't like them, sniff and say no cat ever loves a person, only a place: one of those generally stated facts which is complete nonsense. Anyway, there can be no denying that many famous artists, musicians and writers have kept much-beloved cats; perhaps the mutual admiration is helped by the fact that a cat has no bark to interrupt work!

Kathleen's early liking for the piano was something that did not fade. After receiving elementary lessons at home she was sent to Miss Frances Walker, a Blackburn music teacher with a wide circle of pupils. Miss Walker was herself a pupil of the famous maestro of piano teaching, Tobias Matthay.

And there was always singing. Many of Kathleen's relatives were members of one of Blackburn's choirs, and she took part in choral singing at quite an early age. In those days the only big professional orchestra apart from those in London, was the world famous Hallé in Manchester.

Dr. Herman Brierly, chorus master of the Hallé, was a well-known musical figure in Blackburn. The Ferriers were members of the choir which he founded, later continuing its life under the present title of the Blackburn Musical Society, which flourishes today. Kathleen sang in this choir, later becoming a member of the James Street Congregational Church Choir, along with several of her friends. During this time she studied hard at her piano lessons, and her piano teacher found her an extremely rewarding pupil.

Along with her music, she was happy at school, good at literature, French, Latin and Mathematics; and at home she was part of a devoted and happy family circle. Her father was a great reader, like so many North Country folk, and her elder sister Winifred followed her father in course of time into the teaching profession. But Kathleen progressed so well at her music that in 1924, before she was thirteen, she gained fourth place out of forty-three competitors.

A Bach prelude was one test piece, and in 1925 she played a composition by Debussy among other test pieces in a competition in which she came second out of twenty-six young people.

For much of her life Kathleen was to find herself handicapped by a marked diffidence, an unsureness in her capabilities, which lasted up to the time when she was becoming a famous singer. Again and again this lack of confidence pulled her back from taking first place where piano playing was concerned.

But her diffidence did not prevent her passing, in the same year, her Final examination of the Associated Board of the Royal Academy of Music and the Royal College of Music. This was success indeed, such as seldom came to so young a pupil. There followed a diploma course for teaching and accompanying. All this was not undertaken with the object of her embarking on the hazardous career of a music teacher. The Ferriers wanted their daughter to be able to make full use of her undoubted talent; but though they had grudged nothing in pursuing this end, the times were not propitious for any young girl to launch out in teaching. Unemployment was mounting in the nineteen-twenties, and some safe and certain job had to be considered.

The fees for the piano lessons were a quite considerable expense in a household of modest means; and when Kathleen was fifteen she left High School, so that there should still be enough money for continued music study.

As always in such a case, the mistresses were concerned at her leaving early. It seemed such a waste of a clever pupil. But Kathleen was also a sensible girl, and fully realized that she had to pull her weight in the day-to-day business of earning daily bread. So the fifteen-year-old pianist went to St. John's Lodge private branch telephone exchange to start her training as a telephone operator.

At first she was not happy. The born artist, even long before she or he may be fully aware of their destiny, can be devastatingly unhappy in an ordinary routine or office job. To outsiders this unhappiness can often appear as obstinacy in refusing to settle down to the early adult world after schooldays, or downright laziness combined with a tendency to indulge in daydreams. One can guess that Kathleen never gave people cause to regard her as being resentful. She took the harder side of life with a quiet cheerfulness. And beneath her sweetness of disposition there lay a toughness of fibre and a resilience that asserted itself quite early on. It was not long before she was as popular with the telephone girls as she had been at school.

All this time, under Miss Walker's tuition, Kathleen's musical knowledge and performance matured. At the age of sixteen she entered a very important competition, organized with a blaze of national publicity, by the *Daily Express*. The aim was to reveal teenage talent throughout Britain, and there was promotion of the interests of piano makers—the winner of each area contest to receive an upright piano, value £250. To Kathleen the idea of winning a Cramer piano, an instrument that would be hers alone, was a goal worth striving for with everything she had in her. Every second of practice time was taken up by the test pieces, and it is easy to imagine the alternating hopes and fears that must have possessed her as The Day, 21st November, 1928, drew steadily nearer!

This was the first occasion when the name of Kathleen Ferrier appeared in a national newspaper, but it was only one of many, and it is doubtful if either her friends or relations ever expected her to get really near the top, with so many scores of competitors.

On her journey to Manchester, where the area contest was to be held in the Memorial Hall, Albert Square, she was accompanied by her sister Winifred. Round the corner was the Free Trade Hall where Sir Hamilton Harty conducted the Hallé; we can guess Kathleen must have been much too nervous to take in any details of the big city.

But she gained confidence in watching the competitors on the platform before her own turn; to see their nervousness or strain under the stony-faced judges. There is nothing like realizing the 'other fellow' is more nervous than yourself, to strengthen your nerves. And when Kathleen's turn came, her usual diffidence fell away the moment her hands were on the keyboard.

The judges did not hesitate. They announced that the winner of the area contest was Miss Kathleen Ferrier. She had won her coveted piano, and had also qualified to go forward to the final contest, which was to be held on 1st December, 1928, at the Wigmore Hall.

As Mrs. Ferrier was ill, it was again Winifred who shepherded her young sister down to London.

The following morning they had to go to the Wigmore Hall, and this time Kathleen's usual nervousness swept over her in what one can guess were sickening waves. Cyril Smith and Phyllis Sellick, both destined to become famous pianists and also Kathleen's friends, were among the fellow competitors.

Alas for her hopes, Kathleen was not among the six winners; but she still had the consolation of having won the area competition, and there was the piano which never in a hundred years could she have afforded to buy.

The sisters went to Drury Lane to cheer themselves up. But Paul Robeson's voice stabbed into the reaction Kathleen was going through, and she wept unceasingly. A telegram of sympathy from Miss Walker did nothing to cheer her; and the journey home to Blackburn must have been a subdued one.

But once back, there was the Cramer piano. It was at first exhibited in the window of a music shop, but the day came when, amid rejoicings, it was installed in Kathleen's home. Of course the local press made the most of its new young celebrity. A photograph was published, of quite a plain girl whose best feature was her rather lovely eyes; but there was no hint of the serene beauty that was one day to be hers.

Friends and neighbours were impressed, so were her colleagues of the post office. But Miss Walker had her eyes fixed on a further goal for Kathleen, the preparation of the Licentiateship of the Royal Academy, which lay two years in the future in 1929.

Naturally, a teaching diploma meant a very stiff test. The music set for the practical part of this examination demands a very high degree of both technical and musical ability in order to perform it up to the standard required.

There are also endless scales, arpeggios, etc., of each kind to be performed at the same degree of proficiency and, further, in a multiple variety of ways. Also, the teaching knowledge required covers an extremely wide field and includes 'Form' (the term used when dealing with the different methods of construction employed when writing the various types of musical composition). The questions given both in the written and vocal parts of the examination cover every imaginable facet of teaching—including a thorough knowledge of the rudiments of music: a certain amount of harmony, aural tests, etc.; and also requires that the candidate be prepared to give different alternative methods of dealing with any practical problem (including the fingering of passages given) which may arise when teaching, according to the type, age and ability of the pupil in question.

It can be clearly seen from the above, that gaining this diploma is no mean task, and that it can only be accomplished by consistent hard work of a very high standard maintained over a considerable period of time.

So here was study in plenty for the next two years. But in June 1930, two months after her eighteenth birthday, she was appointed as probationary telephonist at a commencing salary of nineteen shillings a week. And before long—this was in the days when telephones did not have dials, and when you lifted the receiver a feminine voice trilled 'Number-r-r, please!'—she became known as the girl with the lovely voice.

At this time she was fond of dancing and a keen tennis player; the popular songs of the day she could get at one hearing, both words and music. As well as her piano playing, she continued with her choir singing. One of her first small parts was in an amateur production of *Elijah*, when she sang the middle part in the trio 'Lift thine eyes'. At twenty she sang with the James Street choir the solo 'God shall wipe away all tears' from *Gaul's Holy City*, at that time a popular work, now rarely or never heard.

Meanwhile the intensive piano study bore the golden reward of her L.R.A.M. diploma in 1931—the A.R.C.M. having been won in 1929. The L.R.A.M. was distinction indeed at nineteen.

Kathleen had now qualified to start as a music teacher, with a fair prospect of enough pupils to enable her to make a modest career. But she went on with her post office work, probably because the inducement of a pension was to be weighed against the very real uncertainties of music teaching at a time when the industrial slump was at its height. With so many unemployed, and money short everywhere, second thoughts were needed before throwing over a safe job, even an irksome one.

Her professional singing career was still eight years away in the future; but at this time she was singing, either solo or in choirs, and all the time learning. What was more, learning so well and with such good results that her friends began to say things like 'You ought to go in for singing seriously' or 'You should be on the concert platform'.

But money was required for concert training, and in March 1931, William Ferrier retired from his head-mastership. This reduced the family's already modest income, and there could be no thought at that time of giving up the post office job.

If Kathleen still was not really happy in her work, she was not the sort of person to show it. Everyone in contact with her always spoke of her sunny humour and good spirits. Peals of laughter coming from the tele-phonists' rest room usually meant that young Miss Ferrier was entertaining her colleagues with the latest joke or funny story.

If she could not realize her ambitions to be a concert singer, music was nevertheless a thread of gold running through the not very bright colours of her everyday life. She won a gold medal at the Liverpool festival in May 1930, and in April of the same year gained first prize at Lytham. In July her first piano broadcast came out from the Manchester studios. Although she still had four more years of her life in Blackburn, and eight before singing became a really big part of her life, slowly but surely music was more and more claim-ing her for its own.

CHAPTER

3

AT school both Kathleen and her sister Winifred had been Girl Guides, and school leaving had not meant the end of Kathleen's interest in the movement. She joined the Guides' dramatic society, and this in its turn led to her taking a step which was to have considerable significance to her future career. Miss Ida Shaw ran a school of dramatic art in Preston New Road not far from the Ferrier home. Kathleen started to go there for elocution lessons one evening a week. She kept up her attendance for a year, learning clear diction and voice control; and how to make the best use of her vocal chords for both stage and everyday purposes. At this time she was a pianist, and only incidentally a singer; but this was the first step towards the training that would one day bear such glorious results.

While studying with Miss Shaw, Kathleen was given the part of King Arthur in a Girl Guides' play. On the last night one of the curtains caught fire, and there might have been one of those once all too familiar disasters in a hall where amateur dramatics took place, but luckily there were no casualties, though the flames spread rapidly and the younger children in the audience

began to panic. Kathleen helped by calmly announcing there was nothing to get worried about. The fire was soon put out by the Guides, but naturally the local press went to town on the story and Miss Kathleen Ferrier found herself giving her first interview!

By this time Kathleen was a young woman of twenty, with the teenage years in the past. Being a gay and attractive person, there was no shortage of young men who wanted to squire her. But, very wrapped up in her music, she kept them at a cool arm's length, until she eventually met one who—though he worked in a bank and was not a musician—seemed to have many interests in common with her. She became engaged to Albert Wilson, who also worked in Blackburn.

During the beginning of her two years' engagement she entered her first singing competition, and promptly won a prize. There were plenty of other musical occasions in her life at this time, but one highlight was her playing accompanist to Isobel Baillie in a song recital from the B.B.C.'s Manchester studios. It was the beginning of Kathleen's long friendship with the well-known soprano.

Kathleen celebrated her twenty-first birthday in April 1933. It is strange to note how many musical people, singers, conductors, and composers have been born under the constellation of Taurus, towards the end of April and the beginning of May; Kathleen's birthday was on the 22nd.

Then suddenly her life in Blackburn changed completely; in the early months of 1934 she was transferred to Blackpool. This meant a considerable upheaval; a move away from friends and neighbours she had known all her life. Home was replaced by living in 'digs', and an entirely new set of people in her post office career.

Blackpool, centre of the 'Wakes Weeks', and a holiday resort for hundreds of thousands of people every year, has a brash, loud, vivid life of its own. Some hate it, some loathe it—but it is impossible to ignore it as a place! One may guess that the shrieking enjoyments of the holiday-makers did not appeal to Kathleen, but as usual she faced up to her changed life and made the best of things. In this she was helped by being lucky enough to find congenial friends in Marion Parr and her mother who lived in Blackpool. They were musical people, and during Kathleen's two years in the town the Parr home became a haven of kindness. Southerners are apt to sneer at the tag of 'The warm-hearted North'—'where people actually speak without being introduced, my dear!'—but that warmth is no myth, as anyone who has experienced it can testify.

Amateur dramatics did not stop for Kathleen after her move to Blackpool. With Marion Parr and another girl they formed a trio, singing as male impersonators at social gatherings. She made a dashing young man, complete with monocle and topper and male evening dress, and a signature tune, rather reminiscent of the Western Brothers who were first famous in the thirties, 'Three perfectly priceless old things'. It was an early example of Kathleen's talent for brilliant mimicry.

The usually rather dull post office suddenly became a much more exciting place to work in during 1935. An idea which had been under discussion for some time previously was being carried into effect by the authorities. This was the now taken-for-granted 'speaking clock'.

Every paper carried headlines about it, and the question, 'Who will be the Girl with the Golden Voice?' excited nation-wide interest. A national competition for telephone operators would finally choose the voice to be recorded on the delicate and intricate machinery that would respond to the dialling of TIM. The actual sentence spoken was deceptively simple: 'At the third stroke it will be ten forty-five and thirty seconds'.

Kathleen and her friend Marion Parr decided, more as a joke than anything else, to enter the regional stage of the contest. Kathleen's nervousness let her down, and she only reached the local test, but Marion Parr was much more successful. Not only did she pass the Blackpool test, but she went on to win at Preston, Manchester and finally travelled up to London.

The final winner was a London girl, Miss Jane Cain, but Marion had done wonderfully to get so far, and although she was very disappointed, getting so far made it something to be proud of for Blackpool.

On her return she found that Kathleen, herself and another girl had been chosen to demonstrate at a post office exhibition. Kathleen and the other girls had to welcome members of the public and answer questions about the telephone service, which at that time was rapidly extending.

Kathleen's marriage, and the buying of a house in Warton near Kirkham, finally ended her post office career. She was now twenty-four, and it seemed that her life was finally mapped out along quiet lines, with music mostly a hobby. Certainly a brass plate appeared on her front gate, 'Kathleen Wilson, L.R.A.M., A.R.C.M.', announcing herself as a teacher of the piano, but the lessons were as much to keep her own piano playing from rusting as to help with the family income. There was never any question of her going all out and striving to gather in a lot of pupils in order to make a living out of it.

A few months later Albert Wilson's bank sent him to Silloth, in Cumberland. They had only lived in Warton for a very brief period, but Kathleen had made friends there, as she was always destined to do among the famous as well as the obscure.

CHAPTER

4

It was the first time Kathleen had lived outside Lancashire. The move to the Bank House in Eden Street, Silloth, where her husband was now manager, meant a sojourn among strangers. But the Cumbrians, quieter and more reserved than the volatile Lancastrians, were not destined to remain strangers for long. Kathleen was to find very soon that her lot had been cast among folk who, once they had become her friends, remained her friends for life. And the little town of not much more than 3,000 inhabitants, opened new vistas of beauty for Kathleen. The harbour of Silloth, with its coming and going of shipping, sometimes from far distant ports; the view across the Solway Firth to the Scottish mountains soaring away into the dim blueness of far horizons; the scent of pinewoods that lay fragrant on the sunlit air in that summer of 1936, all were very different from anything Kathleen had ever known. There were lonely beaches to bathe from in warm weather, and the sea was excitingly near wherever one went in the town or surrounding countryside.

During the tourist season, there would come carnival

time, when tourists from the not distant Lake District would come to see the Cumbrian style wrestling and other sports. Cockermouth, and its associations with Wordsworth, including the famous Lakeland poet's birthplace, was a car drive away, and a little farther on was the Northern tip of the Lake District at Bassenthwaite with its long lake amid wild romantic scenery, the soaring peaks of Skiddaw in the distance.

A really long day's outing would bring Keswick within reach, and Derwentwater, with some of the most beautiful scenery in England round Borrowdale; the rolling fells with the young green bracken in spring, or the blazing purple of ling and gold of gorse in late summer and autumn. And below Cockermouth lay the bleaker grandeur of Crummock Water and Buttermere, all the country immortalized by Hugh Walpole in his 'Herries' novels.

Nearer at hand was Carlisle, with its cathedral and the ancient grandeur of a border city. There were fine shops to be visited, and above all concerts and theatres, for Carlisle has always had a musical life of its own. In fact Cumberland is the birthplace of music festival competitions, and music plays a big part in the lives of Cumberland people.

There was a music society and a choir in Silloth itself, while the coast towns to the south all had choral or musical societies—Workington, Whitehaven, Millom, Maryport, and inland Cockermouth. These were the places that were to hear Kathleen's voice during the next year or so, along with Carlisle and Egremont. Long before the rest of the world was to recognize her wonderful voice, Cumberland knew all about her brilliance, both as a pianist and a coming singer. Her new Cumbrian friends were soon telling her, just as her old Blackburn friends had insisted: 'You must go in for singing—you must take it up really seriously!'

Yet at this time her life was very much that of any other young married woman, with an added talent for music. She ran the house at first without any help, she liked cooking and domesticity, in fact one can guess she found it all a welcome change after the rut into which she had fallen at Blackpool in a job which, however congenial the people she worked with, she had never found anything but irksome. Her status as a bank manager's wife assured her of plenty of social activities, one of which was golf. Having joined Silloth golf club she took up the game in earnest. Her love of golf remained with her for the rest of her life; and in the days when fame and never-ceasing hard work demanded an occasional outlet and relaxation, she was at her happiest on any good golf links.

In March 1937 she entered for the Carlisle Festival—not only as a pianist this time, but also as a contralto. She had had no further singing lessons, but through her own efforts, and with the continual choral or musical society appearances she had made in the places mentioned above, her voice had very greatly improved. Warm sincerity combined with a rich fullness made people who had once heard her want to listen to her singing again and again.

One of the principal judges at the festival was Maurice Jacobson who came from London, and whose good opinion had very often meant much in the careers of promising musicians. At the finale—the festival went on for a week—winners in the various classes mostly performed in the city's theatre. A silver rose bowl was the prize for the best singer of all, and the judges had no hesitation in awarding it to Kathleen. Maurice Jacobson observed that the winner had a very beautiful voice, one of the finest they had heard. His opinion was wildly applauded, and Kathleen not only had another trophy for her growing collection, but her services as a singer were in immediate and increasing demand all over the county.

In December, a few months later, she took part in *Messiah*, a work in which she was to become world famous. The performance was given at Maryport by the Brow Street Methodist Church Choir. Their conductor, Mr. Wilfred Brinscombe, had engaged her after hearing her at the Festival. This was a memorable occasion, as being the first time Kathleen was paid a fee, which she gave to charity. Afterwards she was to sing with the same choir many times, until fame and world demand took her far from Cumberland.

Kathleen was winner of the Gold Cup at the Workington Festival in 1938. It was awarded for solo voice, and again the judges were tremendously impressed with the power and beauty of her singing. Only a month after this she won a gold medal at the Millom festival, but more than cups or medals she must have treasured the golden opinions she was winning from all sorts of people.

Towards the end of the same year she sang at a charity concert given in Workington Opera House. The concert was called 'Artists You Might Never Have Heard', and in the audience was a 'talent spotter' from the B.B.C. Mr. Cecil McGivern, who has since become very well known, was at that time compering a programme due to be broadcast from Newcastle where he was a producer. It can be well imagined that a B.B.C. man looking for worth while material was fairly bored after listening to the usual run of singers, pianists, choirs, etc. But when a girl in a white dress stood revealed by the curtains, and started to sing 'Ma Curly-headed Babby'—well, that was a very different story. And without hesitation he engaged Kathleen for her first broadcast.

Both Kathleen's parents had been among the audience at Workington, and the pleasure of looking forward to the broadcast was mingled with their delight at the producer's verdict and decision to engage their daughter for the B.B.C. programme. But Mrs. Ferrier was never to hear Kathleen on the air. She became seriously ill, and early in 1939 she died, only a few weeks before the broadcast in February.

Kathleen sang 'Mighty like a Rose', 'Ma Curly-headed Babby', and 'A Perfect Day' with Millom Male Voice Choir. She had to go with the other performers by motor coach to the Newcastle studios, and did not get back to her own home—the farthest point away from Newcastle of any of the performers—until four o'clock the next morning. She took part in seven other programmes at Newcastle after this, but on later occasions she went by car, a car which her father had bought for her.

Kathleen had always been devoted to her father, who was now seventy-one and had gone to live with his elder daughter Winifred in London. Both her sister and father took great interest in her dawning career, and Miss Ferrier tells us that she had been constantly urging Kathleen to seriously consider making music her future career.

As Miss Ferrier's flat was small and the old gentleman was alone for much of the day, owing to his daughter's work at teaching, Kathleen suggested that he should join her and her husband at Silloth. It was an arrangement that worked out very well, for Mr. Ferrier loved watching the shipping at the docks, and the bustle of arrival and departure from the harbour. This, with his pride and pleasure in his daughter's musical gifts, gave him an interest and happiness in life which, with less considerate children, would have become lonely and empty after his wife's death.

What with being in constant demand as a singer, giving a considerable number of piano lessons a week, and her domestic duties, Kathleen's life had become a very busy one. And then in March 1939 she decided to enter yet another Carlisle festival, this time for a trophy presented by the *Cumberland News*. If the Newcastle broadcast had been a significant milestone in her life, this particular competition was destined to be an even bigger one, for one of the judges was Dr. J. E. Hutchinson of Newcastle. With his fellow judge, Dr. Armstrong Gibbs, Dr. Hutchinson awarded Kathleen the trophy—a rose bowl—for her singing of 'Alterseelen' ('All Souls Day') by Richard Strauss. Dr. Hutchinson has said that Kathleen's singing was untutored but nevertheless made a tremendous impression on himself and his fellow judge 'while the beauty of her voice stood out like a beacon'.

For the next three years Dr. Hutchinson was to coach Kathleen's voice, and it so happened that she had put herself into the best hands she could have wished for in the North of England at that time.

In April she called on Dr. Hutchinson at Newcastle, and lessons were duly arranged. He passed through Carlisle every week, and Kathleen was able to have lessons with him there—lessons that continued from autumn 1939 until the end of 1942 when she was to move to London with her father.

It is probable that if it had not been for the war Kathleen would not have been able to have those lessons, as Newcastle is eight miles from Silloth; but when war broke out in September 1939, a school, one of those where Dr. Hutchinson taught music, evacuated to Keswick in the Lake District. He travelled to this school once a week, and as his way lay through Carlisle, Kathleen was able to have her lessons.

1939 was a shadowed year; one in which every remaining moment of pleasure and happiness was snatched under the looming menace of Nazi Germany. Some hoped passionately that the coming crash could in some way be avoided, others knew that war was inevitable. In countless ordinary homes that summer of sunlight and cloud was the last they would ever know as a united family. Either death in action, or the scattering of families in the coming years would break the circle for ever. So it was to be with Kathleen's marriage. Her husband was called up in 1940, and though they were to meet again, the dazzling success of her career meant that music was to claim her, heart and soul. Years later, with the ruin of war between, they separated—the end of a dream of a home and children that was not to be.

When the Bank House at Silloth had to be given up, Kathleen and her father moved to Carlisle, and they were joined by her sister who was teaching there. Their house was very small, but in those days a single room away from the cities likely to suffer from raids, was more precious than gold. Silloth had a large aerodrome, so that even if Kathleen had wanted to go on living there, R.A.F. personnel took every available inch of the town and its surrounding billets.

But war did not stop Kathleen's urge to pursue the career which was only now just beginning to really open before her. If so much of her life was constant striving and then all too brief a flowering, at least she was destined to give pleasure and in return receive the love and affection of untold thousands; a destiny which it is given to few to fulfil in such overflowing measure.

CHAPTER

5

An icy January brought in the dark year of 1940; the long, dreary months known as the 'phoney war', followed in a May of such blazing weather as has never been known since, by the nightmare *blitzkrieg* that rolled over Europe, enslaving one country after another. In England it was as if all nature had combined to show the men and women about to undergo the greatest ordeal in their history, how lovely and how worth fighting for was every acre of flowering countryside. The foaming masses of red and white hawthorn, the larks singing in the fields, the wild roses budding amid the darker green of coming June, all were there to welcome the weary men brought off from the flaming beaches of Dunkirk. The North as yet knew little of the war; though through many camps and hospitals in Southern England the tragedy of France's fall, which so nearly resulted in Britain's army being wiped out, was brought grimly and tensely home.

But long before autumn, as the skies of London glowed crimson with an inferno of sirens, alarm bells and crashing masonry, Hitler's *Luftwaffe* turned its attention to the provinces. Liverpool was to be devastated for miles, Newcastle and the north-east coast were seldom to know a day without hit and run raids, and many nights of heavy bombardments. Kathleen's first big engagement after she had started her lessons with Dr. Hutchinson was a performance of *Messiah* which he was conducting at the City Hall at Newcastle. The night before she was due to sing Kathleen suffered one of those anxiety dreams, only too common at that grim time. In her dream the hall had been burnt down, and so vivid was the vision that when she found that it was still standing, she burst into tears of relief.

At this time Kathleen was building up a repertoire of vocal works by Handel, Purcell, Schubert, with many traditional airs and folk songs as well. The days of music as a hobby were far behind her now; it was a matter of practice, practice and yet more practice— hour after hour every day. Perhaps music, to a greater extent than any other career, requires more consistent concentration from anyone who wishes to be even moderately successful. Whether they sit at the piano for hours of practice or whether it be the singer striving always for a better, a wider range, a more mature and more glorious voice, there can never be any ending to it. There is no room for the person who wishes to take an easy path in life. Music is like learning a language; you are never done, and the more advanced you become, the more you realize how little you know. In fact, music is perhaps the greatest language of all—the only truly universal tongue.

Kathleen had never been afraid of hard work; her early success at the piano showed that. But from this point on in her life, mere hard work became a constant,

32

relentless striving after perfection—a determination, nonetheless determined for being quiet, or hidden under a gay, laughing exterior.

And then came the first offer of concert work away from home. It was through the C.E.M.A., the Council for the Encouragement of Music and the Arts, which did such sterling work all over the country in wartime, bringing music to people who otherwise would have had none. Kathleen was told, after her voice had been heard by Eve Mitchell, that she could have any amount of work if she was prepared to go where she was sent at any time under any circumstances. This meant being away from home a great deal, and often singing under circumstances of acute discomfort, sometimes in most unsuitable surroundings, such as barns or bandstands. But Kathleen's sister was able to look after Mr. Ferrier, and urged her on to go right ahead with her career. And from this point Kathleen's life takes on a new tempo—one broken by the ceaseless rhythm of countless railway trains up and down the country.

It was not a comfortable life. Very much the reverse, in fact. Travel in wartime was a particularly horrible nightmare; with halts of up to two hours and more, perhaps in a big city station with an alert on and gunfire thundering through the blackout, with unpleasantly close 'crumps' of bombs shaking the track beneath the train. The carriages were often unheated in the most freezing weather, or crowded with troops so that a journey of several hundred miles might be taken perched on a suitcase in a draughty corridor. Food was either non-existent or half cold and extremely unpalatable; and the rudeness of wartime railway police and staff could be appalling. The faintest complaint was apt to be retorted upon by the maddening words: 'Don't you know there's a *war* on?' It was no wonder that sometimes tempers, frayed by sleepless nights, were apt to flare over the most trivial subjects.

But one can guess that Kathleen took all these war-time discomforts in her stride, meeting them with her usual good humour and patience. Of course, all her travelling was not unpleasant. Kindness and tolerance were to be met with in the most unexpected people and places. Rudeness very often came from civilians with an inflated idea of their own importance in some small wartime job, the sort of folk who are equally selfish in war or peace. Servicemen mostly concealed their boredom or fed-upness under a cheery philosophy which, where those who strove to entertain them were concerned, blossomed into gratitude, even when the artists were—as they could be—extremely mediocre.

Kathleen also sang to numerous audiences of school children around this time. Mostly these were on their best behaviour—but not always; and Kathleen had no hesitancy in bringing an awkward school audience to heel if they showed signs of getting out of hand and spoiling things for those who really wanted to listen to music.

Towards the end of 1941 Kathleen was engaged to sing in *Messiah*, a performance that took place at St. Anne's-on-Sea. While she was rehearsing, she slipped over to Blackpool to hear the Hallé orchestra conducted by Sir Malcolm Sargent. Luckily for Kathleen, it happened that Alfred Barker, leader of the B.B.C. Northern Orchestra heard her in *Messiah*, and he engaged her for a broadcast concert from the Manchester studios. Alfred Barker introduced her to Sir Malcolm Sargent, who promised to hear her. But a great conductor leads a busy enough life at any time, and at this period of the war Sir Malcolm—then Dr. Sargent—was tremendously heavily engaged in work. Only in May 1942 did Kathleen go to a Manchester hotel and sing to him. She learned that he was of the opinion she had a great future. But she must go and live in London if she really wanted to succeed in her chosen career.

And it was at this point that something very important indeed happened; something which forwarded Kathleen's journey to success perhaps more quickly than any single step she had hitherto taken. Sir Malcolm Sargent contacted her, and said that he was writing about her to Ibbs & Tillett the famous concert agents. The result was that the agents arranged an audition at the Wigmore Hall in London during July 1942.

It was a long time since Kathleen had played the piano here in a competition final, a raw and untried girl. But on this occasion she was probably just as nervous, for she had to play to a practically empty hall. But the result of the audition was that Mr. Tillett put her name on his books, and the great step forward had been accomplished. From being a provincial professional singer, of whom no one in the metropolis had really heard, she had now gained a manager in London.

After this things began to happen fast. Obviously Kathleen could not remain up in Carlisle if she wanted to reach the heights of fame; also Dr. Hutchinson had

helped her so much that she was ready to go further under other tuition. She was continuously practising, putting forth all her energy into singing, singing and more singing; her whole life had by this time become dedicated to her voice.

But Kathleen never allowed ambition to harden her. Always she was a gay, warm person, ready to joke and laugh, enjoy a game of cards, go out on window shopping expeditions to look at the eighteenth century furniture, the old glass and antiques she adored, and for which she had a natural good taste. The day was not yet when she could afford to buy lovely things for herself; but there were museums and art collections in many of the cities she visited. Her interest in painting was later to develop into an actual taste for doing pictures of her own. Like Sir Winston Churchill and many other people whose daily task brought them great strain and concentration, she was to find in painting an ideal 'rest therapy', a hobby which enabled her to relax after some particularly arduous concert tour or broadcast.

At this time Kathleen, who had left school when she was fourteen, had never had a great deal of opportunity for reading; that also was a pleasure that lay in the future, though she was never in any true sense of the word a bookish person. She knew little about musical history, and though she had a good deal of experience of oratorio, she had never visited a first-class production of opera. She knew neither German nor Italian, both languages very necessary for a singer. She had a smattering of French, and perhaps remembered enough Latin, again from her schooldays, to

37

recognize the sense of Latin words to sacred music when she came to sing them. But these shortcomings were more than made up for by a willingness to learn, and an eager interest in every task she undertook. In 1943 she knew some *Lieder* in English, though she had yet to learn it in its native German. *Lieder* is a certain type of singing which requires very specialized treatment on the part of the singer; and for great musical interpretation a voice of exceptional emotional power is essential.

The end of 1942, produced two happenings of the greatest importance to Kathleen's future career. The first of these was her singing with Roy Henderson in Mendelssohn's *Elijah* at Runcorn. They had not met before, and the famous singer and teacher who was destined to coach Kathleen's voice to its ultimate glory, was not particularly impressed.

Poor Kathleen was nervous, as in those years she so often was. She sang correctly but without feeling, and she held her music close before her face. She found it difficult to memorize and was terrified of forgetting her lines. Roy Henderson thought the basic quality of her voice was something out of the ordinary, but it was far too dark and sombre, with no light and shade in interpretation. Afterwards he told her bluntly: 'Very good, my dear, but you must learn your work.'

Kathleen never minded being 'told things straight'. And when on the following day, which was Christmas Eve, they met on the platform at Crewe, that universal meeting point for concert artists, he asked her to join himself and another pupil, a soprano, in the carriage, and they travelled down to London together. Kathleen told Mr. Henderson that she was going to make her future home in London. They talked together, and she realized the truth of his criticisms, storing them away in her mind for further thought. The results of this first meeting and his friendly advice we shall see later.

This move to London was the second big occurrence at the close of 1942. After Kathleen had been put down in Mr. Tillett's books, her sister Winifred, knowing that financial security and a background would be essential for success, decided that she must get a teaching post in London where she had been before the move to Carlisle at the outbreak of war. Luckily an offer came along of its own accord almost immediately. It was then decided that a home must be found in London, both for the two sisters and their father, and the answer turned out to be a flat in Hampstead.

London was terribly scarred by the blitzes, but at this time raids had died down for the moment. No one (except for a few very top people in the know) dreamed of Hitler's flying bombs: those monstrosities were still an unpleasant surprise held by the future. Anyway, life had to be carried on, and the Ferriers had not the slightest hesitation in leaving the greater security of the North for London.

So while Winifred managed the move from the London end, Mr. Ferrier stayed with friends until the new home should be ready. Kathleen was particularly busy that December, singing in *Elijah* as already mentioned, and then in *Messiah* up in Edinburgh.

On Christmas Eve Kathleen finally found herself in a large, draughty flat, uncomfortable for the moment and up fifty steps—twenty to the building entrance, and thirty more to their own front door. Frognal Mansions, a gloomy, high old building must have been wildly difficult to keep warm under fuel rationing conditions; and fixing up black out curtains may be guessed to have been something of a nightmare.

But there they were, for better or worse. What would the future hold? Was it to be success or failure for Kathleen after this bold step? The answer was not long in coming.

CHAPTER

6

DURING the war years there had not been a great deal of music available to the people of Great Britain. Many halls and theatres had been knocked out or badly damaged in the bombing. And then in blacked-out London Dame Myra Hess stepped into the breach with her tremendously popular lunchtime concerts at the National Gallery. The most tragic loss of all, not only for Londoners but for music lovers all over the world, was the Queen's Hall, that delightful home of Sir Henry Wood's Promenade Concerts. The famous Hallé home, the Free Trade Hall in Manchester went too—but that has been rebuilt. But the Queen's Hall site, after a Henry Wood Memorial Fund and a faithful promise of rebuilding, is now a car park; and Londoners have either to go out to the Albert Hall, or across the Thames to the Royal Festival Hall, which may be all very well in its way, but is no proper replacement for the Queen's Hall.

So it was no wonder, that after years of musical dearth, people gratefully flocked to Dame Myra Hess's concerts. It was at one of these that Kathleen made her London début with Roy Henderson in the spring of

1943, before a large and interested audience. She was very nervous over the ordeal, but came through it successfully. She was finding that work was coming along with satisfying regularity, so that already the move to London was being justified. Her reputation was growing with every month—once people had heard her sing, they wanted more and more.

Business engagements took her all over the country, and this meant renewed travelling with all its wartime discomforts. Only when she was very famous and felt that she deserved the extra comfort and peace in which to concentrate on the preliminary work of going over scores and other 'chores' which had to be attended to before a concert, did she go first class. At this time she not only travelled uncomfortably, but had often to put up with unheated and badly provisioned hotels, with all-too-often inhospitable managements. Only anyone who has experienced it can realize quite the depths of the surly 'take it or leave it' service that too many British hoteliers sank to in those years. If Kathleen grew to loathe the sight of tasteless sandwiches and soggy cakes, or half cold, badly cooked meals, who could blame her for disliking life in wartime hotels. It was wonderful to get back home, where at least the best was made of the meagre rations allowed by the dreaded ration books, with their horrible pages of differently coloured squares, without which not enough could be bought to keep one alive.

Kathleen had been thinking about Roy Henderson's good advice to her, and one day in February 1943, while he was teaching between concert engagements at the Royal Academy of Music, Kathleen suddenly turned up with the request, 'Please may I have some lessons?'

Here it is best to quote Roy Henderson's own words:

At the beginning of her first lesson I asked her to sing something of her own choice. She selected Schubert's 'Erlkönig' [The Erl King] in an English translation, as at that time she had not sung in German. I felt at once that here was a voice with which I would have to tread warily. It was so naturally good. Dr. Hutchinson, of Newcastle-on-Tyne had been her previous teacher and had instilled in her a feeling for music, a horror of any sound which was in any way tight or gripped, an easy-flowing tone, and a tongue which kept out of the way at the back of her throat. She had learnt to relax. It was a splendid basis on which to develop. . . .

It takes about seven years to make a singer, provided the material is there, and Kathleen proved no exception. The fact that she became the greatest [singer] of our time was due not to the teaching but to herself. The same teaching can be given to a hundred different people, but the final result is never the same. . . . *

Here Roy Henderson is too modest. However true his words, it is also true that if it had not been that Kathleen was fortunate enough to put herself unreservedly in his hands, it is unlikely that she would ever have fully developed her personality, both musical and

*Kathleen Ferrier, A Memoir, edited by Neville Cardus (Hamish Hamilton, 1954).

otherwise, to the extent she did. When she first went to him, she could not give light and shade to a part; could not read without a score in front of her; could not move on or off a platform; and her horror of showing any emotion was still stifling her dramatic powers.

All this he taught her; and though neither knew it at the time, they were to work together for nearly a whole decade. Countless hours of arduous training lay in the future, the sort of concentrated hard work and perfect collaboration between master and pupil that is only possible when the pupil is willing to strive ceaselessly after perfection.

Towards the end, the teacher became an adviser; but again we find that where other singers might have—justifiably—rested on their laurels, Kathleen never did so. It was Roy Henderson who told her to read as many books as she could get hold of on musical subjects, and this too she faithfully followed out.

Until the end of her life he was to be 'My Prof' to Kathleen, and how deeply we are all in his debt can best now be judged by listening to Kathleen's records.

Very early on their friendship ripened, and Roy Henderson has a story which shows how quickly he made up his mind to get the best out of his new pupil. He had been to supper at Frognal Mansions and they were all washing up after the meal—Winifred at the sink, Kathleen on the other side of the kitchen. It was a time of wartime scarcity in crockery as in most other things, and Mr. Henderson was somewhat startled to see Winifred send the dishes spinning across the kitchen,

44

all shining wet and slippery, to be deftly caught by a laughing Kathleen, ready with a wiping up cloth. Seeing how neither of the sisters dropped a single plate and watching the zest with which Kathleen took part in the 'turn', Roy Henderson made up his mind there and then, that this tremendous vitality must somehow be got into her singing. Here was a very different lass from the nervous, expressionless young woman who sang with her music held up before her eyes!

And sure enough—to look forward into the future—he had her interpreting successfully by 1945; and by 1947 she was so far advanced in *Lied* with him that Mr. Henderson sent her to Hans Oppenheim. Mr. Oppenheim gave her further tuition, and then Mr. Henderson again took her in hand for the presentation. When one remembers that it takes seven years to make a good singer, this was indeed swift progress.

In March 1943 Kathleen went down to the picturesque old town of Lewes to sing at a small concert there. With its steep hill, fascinating old buildings, its ruined castle and nearness to the coast, Lewes is one of loveliest places in Sussex, and this occasion was memorable for two happenings. It was the first time she had sung the lovely aria 'Che faro' from Gluck's *Orpheo e Eurydice*; and it was also the first time she had ever been accompanied by Gerald Moore.

Now Mr. Moore is a world famous accompanist, and also a great artist and musician in his own right; only he can count the famous singers for whom he has played. And, he told the author, none of them was ever shy in the way Kathleen was. She was absolutely terrified of meeting him; knowing he was on the same train, she shrank back in her carriage, breathing a sigh of relief when he passed her. On arrival she peeped out of her window and waited until he was far down the platform before following. This was just another instance of her nervous unsureness of herself at this stage of her career; a shyness which it must have been agony to overcome.

But after the concert Gerald Moore told her how much he had been impressed by her. This she could hardly believe, thinking he was only being kind; but timidly she begged him to put in a good word for her with Roy Henderson by giving him a favourable report of her singing, and also to mention her to concert agents and the B.B.C. Secretly amused—for he knew this was quite unnecessary with a voice as good as hers—he readily agreed to do so. Her shyness conquered, Kathleen was full of excitement over that first meeting. She said later that it was a revelation to work with him—'He thinks and breathes with me'—and in a very short time they had become great friends; a friendship which was to grow and last all Kathleen's life.

One of the most comforting things about these all-too-brief years of Kathleen's fame is the thought of the true and good friends who brought happiness into her life. Always warmly impulsive, gay and affectionate, Kathleen was quick to respond to kindness and understanding; and it says much for the affection she was capable of inspiring, that not only her personal friends like Ena Mitchell, the Roy Hendersons, the Gerald Moores, and the Christies, Cyril Smith and Phyllis Sellick, or Mr. and Mrs. Alexander Maitland in Edinburgh, but many other people outside the particular circle of her intimates, showed themselves anxious to guide and help her sometimes faltering steps into the fierce limelight of world-wide fame.

The music world is not always patient with uncertain beginners. Rivalry is keen, the struggle for recognition fierce; and when once gained, fame still requires fighting for. A new voice, a rising reputation can be very unwelcome. So it is perhaps all the more surprising that when a girl, shy and not over-confident, came upon the scene unexpectedly, so many in musical circles not only acclaimed her but helped her in every way they could.

Naturally there were certain others, also on their way up, who watched Kathleen's swift progress with jealous eyes. But these were always a minority, and Gerald Moore says that the top-flight singers such as Elizabeth Schwarzkopf, Victoria De Los Angeles and Dietrich Fischer-Dieskau admired her voice tremendously.

Perhaps it was that very shyness and diffidence which disarmed criticism in these early days. Had Kathleen shown that she was pleased and sure of herself, hearts might not have warmed towards her so readily. But she was at all times anxious to learn, eager to listen, and never resentful of correction when she knew it was deserved. And at this time if anyone did tend to be unkind—as newspaper critics sometimes were—she would shrug it off with a smile and a philosophical 'Maybe they were partly right—I must try to do better another time'.

Later, she was to feel a justified exasperation when

critics, English and American, were more than ordinarily fatuous in their pronouncements on her singing; but as yet she was too unsure of herself to distinguish the just notices from the merely foolish.

Everyone seems to agree that at this period Kathleen was inclined to be rather gauche—that is, awkward in her deportment on the concert platform, and terribly shy in her dealings with others. She possessed no hint of the serene, smiling poise and grave beauty which later became so complete a part of her. Yet it is obvious that she did not remain so unsure for very long; all the time she was learning, not only her singing and new music to add to her steadily increasing repertoire, but teaching herself to be everything a great singer should be—relaxed, and with a gracious personality and that indefinable something known as 'finish'.

Clothes, too, were something of a problem at this time. Rationing made things very difficult, and it was essential that she should have a certain number of different gowns for her numerously growing appearances. Here again she was lucky in her sister Winifred, who made many of her dresses. In this way Kathleen could always appear suitably gowned, and so not have to wear the same dress in the same town or city where she had appeared before. Later, she was to enjoy expensive clothes, some specially designed for her; but having always had to work hard for every penny she was never ready to go out and spend a lot on herself, without giving the matter severe thought beforehand. Generous for others, she hardly ever treated herself lavishly to anything she decided she did not really need.

In the March of this year, there was a nasty setback while Kathleen was on a C.E.M.A. tour with Maurice Jacobson as accompanist and Kathleen Moorhouse, the 'cellist. They had to travel up to Scotland in bitter weather, and in 1943 heated trains, even with the thermometer at freezing point, were the exception rather than the rule. Nor was there much chance to warm up in concert halls, which were also either inadequately heated or not heated at all. The audience sat in overcoats on top of all their warmest clothes, but as the platform, especially in the smaller type of hall, was the draughtiest part, entertaining must have often been like a special sort of torture out of Dante's Inferno of Ice!

Under these circumstances, one of the last places to land up in during a spring of east winds and scudding grey cloud, was the east coast city of Aberdeen, with its great tall buildings of grey granite, where the wind comes straight from the North Pole and Scandinavia, across the surging grey-green of the North Sea. But where the C.E.M.A. directed, the singers and musicians had to go, every bit as much on wartime service as if they had been in one of the forces. The winter cold took its toll of Kathleen's never very strong health, and she fell really ill.

She must have been struggling on bravely, for on arrival in Aberdeen it was obvious that she could not continue. Kathleen Moorhouse called in a doctor, who took one look at the patient and ordered an ambulance which took her straight to a nursing home with pneumonia.

For weeks Kathleen lay dangerously ill, wondering

through the haze of her illness whether this was to be the end of her brief life as a singer. But gradually she recovered, and was able to return home to the ministrations of her sister. It was a frail and very delicate Kathleen who came back to London, and obviously she had to have some sort of convalescence before she would again be able to take up the threads of her career. Luckily the cold weather had turned to sunshine, and Kathleen was only too glad to go with her sister and father on a country holiday to Blindley Heath in Surrey, where her health was not long in mending.

By the time she returned to London she was fully recovered, which was specially fortunate, as her first big engagement in London loomed ahead that May. This was no less than a performance of *Messiah* in Westminster Abbey, and she was naturally determined to be at the very top of her form. The solo singers were to perform with the Bach Choir and the Jacques Orchestra, under the conductorship or Dr. Reginald Jacques, who himself had asked her to sing, having been deeply impressed by the beauty and sincerity of her voice.

The performance took place on 17th May, 1943, and it is easy to imagine what Kathleen's feelings must have been on such an occasion. Not only was it a great honour to sing in the supreme shrine of the nation, so mercifully spared from the ravages of war, but the very grandeur and vastness of the sacred auditorium must have been almost overwhelming. Many times down the years since the mighty gathering of musicians for the Handel Commemoration in the Abbey in 1784,

performances of sacred works had been given here;
but the audience on this occasion was not one of wealthy
'fashionables' with a scattering of true music lovers. It
was wartime London that came to listen; members of
the forces, the civil defence men and women, the A.F.S.,
the doctors and nurses, and last but surely not least the
ordinary citizens of a London which had survived
everything that evil had tried to do to break its spirit—
'the terror by night' against which we ask to be pro-
tected in the ninety-first psalm.

And as Handel's great work pealed forth through
choir and transept, to be received diminished but still
glorious even to the far end of the nave, only those
present could afterwards try to give others some faint
idea of the grandeur of it all. *Messiah* in a prosaic
concert hall can be impressive enough. Here in Westminster Abbey, under the sure touch of a conductor
who was one with his performers, it was an occasion to
be remembered always by any who had heard it. What
can Kathleen's feelings have been, we may wonder, as
she stood beneath:

> . . . the high embowed Roof,
> With antique Pillars massy proof,
> And storied windows richly dight,
> Casting a dimm religious light.
> There let the pealing Organ blow,
> To the full voic'd Quire below,
> In Service high, and Anthems clear,
> As may with sweetness, through mine ear,
> Dissolve me into extasies,
> And bring all Heav'n before mine eyes.

51

Perhaps only those closing lines from John Milton's *Il Penseroso* can do justice to this memorable performance. And if today, now her lovely voice is silent for us, we would still experience something of the delight and emotion with which people heard her then, we are lucky in being able to listen on a record to her singing 'He was despis'd', and ourselves thrill to the beauty of her voice.

The music critics were also in the Abbey, in force. In the way of critics, they were not over-enthusiastic in their praise, but there was enough in their reports to give Kathleen very real satisfaction.

Next day *The Times* said:

The Soloists were two established Handelians, Miss Isobel Baillie and Mr. William Parsons, and two new-comers, Miss Kathleen Ferrier and Mr. Peter Pears, both of whom established their right to be of that now not very numerous company.

But some weeks later Ferruccio Bonavia wrote in the *Musical Times* on London concerts which had been held that season:

. . . and finally to Miss Kathleen Ferrier, who sang the alto part in *Messiah* in Westminster Abbey. I shall not easily forget the natural dignity of her style or the purity of her voice.

The natural dignity of her style . . . the purity of her voice. Again and again music connoisseurs were to echo those words during the next few years, while countless thousands of ordinary folk were to add: 'That wonderful voice—it seems to come from another world. . . . There's no one else can sing quite so beautifully. . . .'

Because Kathleen was never to be for the musical few; she was to sing her way into the hearts of men and women in every walk of life, a vast multitude who found joy and pleasure in her singing.

CHAPTER

7

AT this stage of her career Kathleen was constantly adding to her repertoire, and also doing a good deal of travelling in C.E.M.A. concerts. In 1944, during another tour of the Potteries, she shared the solo songs with Peter Pears. Among her own solos were 'Sigh no More' and 'The Fairy Lough', along with Peter Warlock's 'Pretty Ring Time'. There is a record both of this last and another of Peter Warlock's songs, 'Sleep'. All this composer's music has a strange, haunting quality, even in its lighter moments. His real name was Philip Heseltine, and one of his most famous and eerie works was a cycle of songs *The Curlew* with words by W. B. Yeats, the great Irish poet. Peter Warlock died at the early age of thirty-six in 1930, his whole brief life shadowed by tragedy. The lovely purity of Kathleen's voice was well suited to his music, to which only an exceptionally fine singer can ever hope to do full justice, and Peter Pears, Kathleen's fellow soloist on that occasion, has also given a fine rendering of Warlock's 'Yarmouth Fair'.

Kathleen liked the appreciative audiences in the factories and halls of the Potteries. The above-mentioned concert took place at the Victoria Hall, Hanley, with the Etruscan Choral Society who afterwards bought a small hall of their own in a back street in Etruria which they decorated themselves. Seating 130 people, it was opened by Mary Glasgow, C.B.E., head of C.E.M.A., and Kathleen sang later that same year at its opening, with Maurice Jacobson accompanying her. She had taken a keen interest in the project from the start, and she was determined that she would do everything in her power to make the new hall a success. She gave three recitals, taking no fee, and in hardly any time the hall was a going concern financially. Faithful audiences still go there for music, but today there is one big difference: the hall is named after Kathleen in memory of her.

Kathleen sang many works for the first time during her tours of Staffordshire, among them Brahms's Alto Rhapsody. But at the Victoria Hall Concert she did more than sing; she played the piano in the 'Lady of Shalott' set to music by Maurice Jacobson for tenor solo, chorus, strings and piano—and her playing showed that she was as brilliant a pianist as she had ever been. A real 'Klever Kaff', as she liked to laughingly call herself. The name dated from a time some years back when a friend's small son, in thanks for having a button sewn on very quickly, said 'Klever Kaff!' And for ever she signed her letters in this way, and when later she painted for a hobby, each canvas carried 'K.K.' in one corner.

This was a time when she decided to accept offers of all sorts of different work—after all, that was the only and best way in which she could find out what suited her. In 1944 she sang in a concert performance of *Carmen* at Stourbridge. It seems that from the first she had considerable doubts about singing the part, but she finally decided to take it on.

Afterwards she decided that the part simply did not suit her in any way, and she would never try it again, even when later on Carl Ebert wanted her to do it at Glyndebourne, and suggested a special interpretation more suitable to her style. Roy Henderson is of the opinion that she could have done it if she had set her mind to it; but he was uneasy about the *tessitura* and forcing her voice too high.

By 1944 Kathleen quite often found herself singing with artists whose names had been famous for many years. Isobel Baillie the well-known soprano was one, Joan Cross another, and there was Elsie Suddaby who later gave Kathleen a lovely amethyst necklace, which became a great personal treasure very often worn, with the added pleasure of the kindness of its giver.

In this same year Kathleen deputized on several occasions for Astra Desmond, who had been taken suddenly ill. Astra Desmond heard the voice of the girl who took her place, and always gave Kathleen the most friendly encouragement, paying her sincere and generous tributes on the quality of her voice.

But the most important experience that caused her to blossom out at this time was her singing in recitals for music clubs, jointly with Roy Henderson. She also sang on many occasions for his choirs at Nottingham and Bournemouth. These took place in many different parts of the country during the next year or so. They would sit down together on the platform, or stand up together for a joint song; then one would sing, then the other; perhaps the second half would consist of solos from either Kathleen or Roy Henderson himself—folk songs, songs from opera, every type of music that entertained. All the time this was helping Kathleen to interpret songs. And as this is difficult for outsiders to understand and impossible for anyone but an expert to describe, here, again, are Roy Henderson's own words:

. . . We painted pictures conjured up by the song. Everything had its relative position on an imaginary canvas before her. Here would be a tree in full bloom, about which she was singing; lambs playing over there; a stream running away in the distance yonder. . . .

Imagination had to go further than merely seeing things that weren't there. Kathleen learnt to hear and to feel. She heard the fury of the storm in 'Die junge Nonne', the sad song of the nightingale in 'Der Tod, das ist die kühle Nacht'. She felt the cooling breeze on her hot cheeks as she sang about it in 'Suleika', the icy shivering wind in 'Vergebliches Ständchen'. I watched her closely all the time. If she sang the words but failed to use her imagination . . . we would try the passage again and again . . . . *

Roy Henderson told the author that the singers' travels took them into many places and situations, some amusing, some not so funny. Once in Liverpool,

*Kathleen Ferrier, A Memoir, edited by Neville Cardus (Hamish Hamilton, 1954).

in 1944, they arrived at the Philharmonic Hall to find there was no light at all for the concert. The only glimmer came from the back of the piano, and as Roy Henderson explained to the audience, it is not much use going to a concert and being unable to see the singer's expressions. So he made Kathleen stand by him at the back of the piano, and somehow the concert went through. It turned out afterwards that the engineer had gone off, not realizing he would be wanted! There was quite a stir in the press, and a letter of apology afterwards.

Another time, when they were staying in one of the best hotels in Chester, they arrived back late, ravenously hungry, only to be greeted with the news that they were too late for a meal, the kitchens were closed for the night, and the staff had retired. This simply wasn't good enough, so they tramped the streets of the ancient city until, down a winding side lane, they came on a tough little pull-up for carmen. Bravely they plunged in—the light and warmth and scent of food more than compensating for the rough and ready service and cutlery—and were served on enormous plates with one of the biggest meals they had eaten in years. Bacon and beans and eggs, with strong workman's tea. Nothing so satisfying was to be found in any hotel restaurant at that time. Kathleen, who had the knack of making herself at home wherever she happened to be, thoroughly enjoyed herself, and so did her 'Prof'.

Kathleen's sense of fun was never long absent. She was tired of wartime travel in crowded carriages, and on at least one occasion resorted to a joke that kept the compartment in which she and her 'Prof' and fellow singers were sitting, beautifully to themselves.

This was done by the simple expedient of Kathleen leaning out of the open window, and pulling the most hideous faces, twitching her hands and making agonized grunting noises while other travellers gave her one horrified stare and hurried on down the train. There were whispers of 'That poor thing—there must be something the matter with her' or 'What are they doing letting someone mad travel alone?' An extra horrible grimace and wild rolling of her eyes ensured privacy for the whole long journey, and as the train gathered speed Kathleen's companions, who had been keeping their heads down out of sight, straightened themselves up, weak with mirth. It was rather a naughty trick for anyone grown-up to play, but a very effective one!

Back home in London raids had started up again for a while, only to die down into deceptive calm for a few months before the onslaught of Hitler's flying bombs. Like everyone else Kathleen was apt to congratulate herself on still being alive when she woke up to a new day. There was no air raid shelter to the old-fashioned flats at Frognal Mansions, and life must have been more than usually nerve-racking at that unpleasant time when, after an alert had sounded, the all-clear would not go for perhaps days at a time, and one never knew when the next near explosion would rattle or shatter all the windows. At first people threw themselves flat on their faces, but finally cover was only sought for particularly 'nasty' ones, which might mean a bomb much less than a mile away, perhaps only in the next street.

All this, on top of the continued wartime travelling and shortages, could not have helped Kathleen's health, though she seemed well enough at this time.

Towards the close of 1944 she sang for the first time in Elgar's *The Dream of Gerontius*, taking the part of the Angel; a part which Roy Henderson had especially warned her she could not possibly interpret correctly unless she could sing from memory, and not just read the part.

Always, in long works Kathleen had a nightmare fear of forgetting her words, and *The Dream* was a particular bogey to her in this respect. Once up in Silloth she had experienced a momentary black-out in singing 'Where'er you walk', and instead of 'all things flourish where'er you turn your eyes', 'where'er they eat the grass' sprang both into her mind and on to her lips at the same appalling instant. Words that had to be sung twice to an audience that could all too easily hear her clear enunciation. Not unnaturally Kathleen was always scared of the same thing happening again; needless to say, it never did.

In this same year, she had sung with Sir Malcolm Sargent conducting two performances of two of Brahms's *Four Serious Songs* in Sir Malcolm's arrangement, the first in Liverpool, the second in Manchester, which was broadcast. By now she was singing in languages other than her own, and recognized by both critics and public as a truly wonderful contralto. She had broadcasts booked up ahead, and a contract for making gramophone records.

Two of her songs from works she sang in at this time luckily remain with us on records. She had sung many times in Mendelssohn's *Elijah*, and 'O rest in the Lord', one of the most beautiful examples of religious music ever written, may still be heard on one of her records. And an aria Kathleen made specially her own, 'Art thou troubled' from Handel's opera *Rodelinda*, can still be heard. Kathleen had a special liking for Handel, whose works suited her voice to perfection; the singing of the famous Largo 'Ombra mai fu' from the opera *Serse* has been more often sung by great tenors, such as Caruso and Gigli; but no rendering has been more beautiful than that of Kathleen's.

Even now she was in such great demand, Kathleen did not forget the Northern Societies with whom she had sung in earlier days. The Blackpool Co-operative Choral Society's concerts were something to be looked forward to in the time when the town was no longer filled with holiday visitors, and on 15th October, 1944, there was a centenary concert at which Kathleen was once again a soloist. Her songs were very different from those she had sung years before—Schubert's 'An die Musik', and that strange, rather weird work 'The Erl King'. She sang for the same society in February 1945, one of her songs on this occasion being 'Art thou troubled'.

At last the war was swiftly drawing to its long-hoped-for end. All this time Kathleen's husband had been in the army, and later in 1945 he was posted to Singapore. Somehow, after such a long time, their worlds lay more than oceans apart; Albert Wilson and Kathleen decided to go their different ways, and Kathleen now had her singing alone.

When peace was only a few weeks old, Kathleen gave

another series of concerts in factories—this time at Stoke, and it was during this tour that she first met Phyllis Spurr an accompanist new to her. At the end of the tour Kathleen realized that here was someone who exactly suited her own ideas, and whom she also liked personally. This proved the start of an association which ripened into companionship, bringing great pleasure to them both. Phyllis Spurr was to play for Kathleen many times at her concerts, and they made records together. There were also arduous rehearsal sessions in the flat at Frognal Mansions—rehearsals with breaks for cups of tea and talk and laughter, before plunging once more into work. Phyllis Spurr also accompanied Kathleen in her lessons with Roy Henderson, for between recitals there was always something new to be learned, and this meant work, work and more work; learning songs in new languages, getting the full meaning of words and phrases, so that the singer knew them as well as anything in her own language; memorizing new parts and, if they were in manuscript, sight-reading them right through with her accompanist—all these things accompanied the strain of appearing before big audiences and constant travelling. Luckily, Kathleen was now able to afford first-class travel, and the days of excessive wartime discomfort lay behind her. For a busy artist, first-class fares were not a luxury but a necessity that gave more privacy for last-minute detail work, and also might ensure that she arrived at a destination a little less fatigued than she would otherwise have done. By now the number of concerts and oratorio performances in which she was appearing meant staying in literally dozens of different places every few months and travelling many thousands of miles. All this, with foreign tours lying still in the future.

It was in September 1945 that Kathleen sang 'L'Air des Adieux', an aria from the Tchaikovsky opera *Joan of Arc* at a B.B.C. Promenade Concert in the Albert Hall. This was a very different broadcast from those early ones from Northern studios; now millions listened to Kathleen's lovely voice, and the critics were enthusiastic in their praise. In December Kathleen's debut with the Hallé Orchestra in Manchester took place at the King's Hall in Belle Vue pleasure grounds, which was for the present the Hallé's home since the Free Trade Hall had been bombed in 1940. This was again a performance of *Messiah*, but with a choir of six hundred voices, and a packed audience of seven thousand people. Isobel Baillie once more sang the soprano part, and Peter Pears, who had sung with Kathleen in Westminster Abbey, was tenor. Norman Walker was the bass, and with Sir Malcolm Sargent conducting, the most exacting Handel enthusiast could not have asked for better.

Concerts, oratorios, recitals—with audiences constantly wanting more; but fresh experience lay ahead for Kathleen in the coming year. For the first time she was to do more than go on a platform and sing; she was to appear, at long last, in opera.

CHAPTER

8

IN the years before the war, Glyndebourne, the beautiful Elizabethan home of Mr. and Mrs. John Christie had been famous for its small opera house where everything was done on a scale of complete perfection unknown since the days of the German princes and Margraves in the eighteenth and early nineteenth centuries. Production, scenery, orchestras, singers—everything had to be of the best; and it was no wonder that people soon flocked by train and car down to this sleepy village between the Sussex Weald and the Downs, not only from all over England, but from all over the world. The old house was set amid lovely flower gardens that were a blaze of colour, and—when the weather was kind—a summer-scented murmur of birdsong and sun-drenched peace.

Even when the weather was not kind—and all too often British summers turned sulky and refused to add outside stage effects—the small opera house itself was a never-failing pleasure for lovers of good music. Mozart, especially, soared to a degree of perfection unknown anywhere outside Salzburg itself. Seats were expensive, so was the food and wine, but the elegant and fashionable audience, many of whom had set out from the station in London in full evening dress by the light of a summer's afternoon, were only too willing to pay for the novelty and pleasure of opera in the heart of the English countryside.

The house with its mellow brick walls, tall chimneys and ancient windows, was a dream of gracious peace, and a very lovely home, with the taste of its artistic owners in every part of it. But during the war Mr. and Mrs. Christie had made their house a children's home, and there had been no opera for seven years.

There had been a greatly revived interest in music among younger people, many of them packing the concert halls during their periods of leave during the latter years of the war. Symphony concerts, recitals, and oratorio had all been increasingly crowded, while there was an avid interest in opera. But with Covent Garden turned into a dance hall 'for the duration', and with so many theatrical people in the services, scope had been very limited. Among the foremost (if not the foremost) of modern composers was Benjamin Britten, whose first opera had been acclaimed as a work of genius and originality. This was *Peter Grimes* based on the story contained in part of the long poem *The Borough* written by the Suffolk poet the Rev. George Crabbe towards the end of the eighteenth century. Crabbe had known great poverty in his life, and his sympathies always lay with the poor and less fortunate folk of his time. He wrote in a stark and very bare style, but often with passages of considerable power. His descriptions were of his native Suffolk coast, the wild, bird-haunted shores; the crumbling cliffs crashing into the all devouring waters of the grim North Sea; the plight of ship-wrecked mariners in howling winter gales; the sufferings of the sick and old. All this, along with detailed and colourful descriptions of plant life, and strange, often tragic stories of east-coast villages, made Crabbe, as well as the more gentle William Cowper, the herald of a new age of English poetry which was to flower to greatness in Wordsworth and Tennyson—the latter another East Anglian poet.

The story of Peter Grimes, the cruel fisherman who ill-treated his boy apprentices and caused their deaths, was wrought into a powerful opera by Benjamin Britten, himself a Suffolk man, with a libretto by Montagu Slater; and after the work had been greeted with acclaim, there was a demand for a second opera.

This was what Britten was working on in 1945; *The Rape of Lucretia*, taken from ancient classical sources, demanded a singer of exceptional qualities in the name part. This new opera was to be produced at Glyndebourne for its re-opening, and, as in the years before the war, cast and production were to be of the very best.

It so happened that when Kathleen had sung in Westminster Abbey, Benjamin Britten had been one of the audience; he had heard her voice for the first time in that performance of *Messiah*. He was greatly impressed, and when later he was writing his new opera and someone suggested Kathleen Ferrier, he was at once enthusiastic. At first she remained undecided, because though it was a highly flattering offer, she could not help feeling very nervous at the idea of exchanging the concert platform for the opera stage. It meant acting as well as singing, learning a great deal more about moving gracefully, managing entrances and exits, performing naturally in costume, and a score of other details, all of which seemed rather alarming to say the least. Her acting experience was limited to a few appearances in school or amateur productions, nothing at all as a professional. And in any case her natural modesty regarding her talent, made her unsure that she would succeed in doing what the composer and the librettist Ronald Duncan wanted.

But if she succeeded it would be a large-sized feather in her cap. She would become a name to many, particularly those from abroad who had not yet heard of her. Yet the array of well known people with whom she would have to work, made her natural nervousness, always ready to boil up into panic, fill her with the awful conviction that she really would just not be good enough. Although this was not a pre-war international company, but a case of the opera house being lent for the start of the English Opera Group, the cast of Britten's opera was sure to be of outstanding merit. So what should she, Kathleen, decide?

It was no wonder that she had many doubts. Glyndebourne standard was and is fantastically high; for what started years before as a private hobby, had long since been financially assisted by famous commercial firms. The cost of production was enormous, and in these days of taxation, no private purse could possibly have run Glyndebourne as a going concern for long. As in Salzburg, though it was no longer an Austrian Archduke or a German Prince who held the purse-strings, the whole standard of taste and excellence was every bit as demanding as anything produced before eighteenth century royalty.

However, further thought, and the knowledge that there was to be quite a long time in which to rehearse, reassured her a little.

Later on Carl Evert had no doubts about her at all. Roy Henderson, who himself had sung regularly at Glyndebourne in pre-war days, took Kathleen along to a house in Kensington, where Ebert and Sir Thomas Beecham heard her sing. Ebert was at once enchanted with her voice, while Sir Thomas listened in his usual wise, inscrutable way, and then commented, 'Very pretty—very pretty!' Perhaps the great conductor was referring to Kathleen's looks as well as her voice!

There was a dinner party at Hampstead where both Benjamin Britten and his librettist Ronald Duncan were guests. *Lucretia* had been discussed, and the name part was afterwards written largely with Kathleen in mind. Ronald Duncan was soon to become a friend, and Kathleen went down to the Duncans in Devon on several occasions. Ronald Duncan breeds Arab horses, and playing with the children and petting the beautiful horses, one can guess the happiness these holidays brought to Kathleen.

Kathleen who had never seen a first-class opera in her life, now found herself plunged into rehearsals, surrounded by famous names. Eric Crozier was to produce Britten's new work and John Piper to design the sets, while Hans Oppenheim was responsible for the musical preparations; the composer conducted.

It was in May 1946 when Kathleen and her fellow singers finally arrived in the fascinating old town of

Lewes, with its castle ruins and winding streets, its steep hill and lovely ancient inns. Glyndebourne was only a bus ride away, and it was a very welcome change for Kathleen to be going to a charming and peaceful house surrounded by beautiful gardens; to have a room of her own with flowers and a wonderful view from the windows, instead of the usual travelling and hotel life which had become her lot as a concert singer.

Even her nervousness at the prospect of arduous rehearsals, must have been lightened by the knowledge that Glyndebourne was to be her home for some weeks. Instead of living out of suitcases she could at least settle down and not feel there was yet another train to be caught—anyway, for a while.

Kathleen found rehearsals every bit as trying as she had feared they would be; this in spite of the fact that, as she afterwards said in a broadcast, she was helped enormously by the other singers who were all tremendously kind and patient with this beginner with the lovely voice.

The singing was very exacting, but more difficult still was the art of graceful movement; the exits and entrances, the use of gesture so that hands and arms should not appear clumsy. Kathleen herself said later: 'I couldn't believe how difficult it was just to do the simplest arm movements without feeling like a broken-down windmill. . . .' But practice made perfect, as it always does if given enough intelligence and determination, and gradually she found herself improving.

Not that life was all rehearsals—far from it. There was a great deal of spare time, for the cast could not be working continuously. Kathleen, who had always loved beautiful old things, found out the fascination of Brighton's antique and junk shops, and in the evenings there was tennis, or knitting, or madrigal singing. And—which was very important for her at this time— continually being with polished and experienced people from whom she could watch and acquire valuable stage knowledge. Perhaps Glyndebourne was the real beginning of that poise and elegant charm which was so soon afterwards to be added to her own warmth and sweetness.

The opening night came at last, and both the opera and Kathleen were a great success. Ralph Hill wrote in the *Daily Mail* of this great occasion:

> The parts of Lucretia and Tarquinius were sung and acted with great skill by Kathleen Ferrier and Otakar Kraus. . . . Benjamin Britten's music is full of beautiful moments and invokes intense atmosphere. His mastery of subtle orchestral colour and dramatic effects is nothing short of genius.

What a triumph it was for Kathleen to read those words 'sung and *acted* with great skill'! A triumph of fears surmounted, of well-learned knowledge put to effective use. Most of all, it was the greatest step forward yet in her career.

Kathleen did not let success at once give her undue confidence; in fact, she tended to remain shy and diffident all through that first stay at Glyndebourne. The added poise which new experience was bringing her was not yet very evident off the stage.

But a new poise was growing, slowly but surely, and

when in September 1946 the opera went to Holland, Kathleen found herself taking her first trip abroad, and her first steamship journey.

The whole Glyndebourne company were appearing in Amsterdam, and Nancy Evans alternated with Kathleen in the title role. The crossing to the Hook of Holland was a new and exciting experience for Kathleen, who at once fell in love with that land of translucent light and wonderful silvery-blue skies—the same skies that can be seen in the Dutch Old Masters in the world's great picture galleries.

Even to those who do not like flat country, there is always something fascinating about Holland. The dykes and canals amid flower-bright fields, the beautifully neat houses with sparkling paint and windows—so clean that it is really no surprise to learn that the smiling housewives regularly wash their homes outside as well as in (a habit that persists from Flemish ancestry to this day in East Anglian villages!). And although sadly diminished there are still many charming windmills, and always flowers and more flowers, although of course tulip time in the spring is the best season of all to see the fields.

Kathleen at once fell in love with Amsterdam and its tall, graceful seventeenth and eighteenth century houses, the tree-lined canals, a charming shopping centre, and cafés and restaurants which in those days seemed packed with food such as war-starved Britain had not seen for five years.

The Dutch audiences welcomed Benjamin Britten's opera with just as much enthusiasm as had been shown in its native country. They welcomed Kathleen too, and Peter Diamand, the Dutch impresario, wanted to know when she could come again for recitals of her own. Kathleen was to return to Holland again, and always she had the warmest spot in her heart for this, the first country she had ever visited outside her own.

When she came home in November, the golden memories of peaceful Glyndebourne, and being able to remain in one pleasant spot for a time without constant travel, must have given her wistful moments during the months of hard work which followed. She had come down to London in 1942 wondering whether there would be enough work to justify the step she was taking. Now, four years later, it was no longer a matter of hoping for engagements, but of trusting that no more offers would come along and add to the strain of what was by now quite considerable overwork.

She visited Ireland soon after her return from Holland, giving two recitals at Queen's University, Belfast, where she received a tremendous welcome. By this time she was appearing in less concerts and giving more recitals, and she felt that she must still further extend her repertoire, particularly of *Lieder* in German. She knew a certain amount, but needed to widen her experience, and as always turned to her 'Prof', Roy Henderson, for advice. The outcome was, as mentioned earlier, that Roy Henderson sent her to Hans Oppenheim, who agreed to coach her in this extremely difficult art.

The German *Lied* is one of the most perfect of all forms of song, and a really outstanding *Lieder* singer is rare. At its best the artistic aim is beauty of expression rather than vocal 'fireworks'—the piano part being equal in importance to the vocal. But the singer who wishes to attain true excellence, and who is not a German, has an arduous task before her. The greatest composers of *Lieder* are Schubert, Brahms, Schumann and Wolf, but to these masters Kathleen added a more recent composer, Mahler.

Kathleen was to become passionately devoted to the works of Mahler, and her interpretation of his *Kindertotenlieder* is truly wonderful *Lieder* singing. There was something in the wild, romantic beauty and often unearthly motif of his work which fascinated her; and indeed anyone, even a listener without knowledge of this form of music, cannot fail to be moved by the power of 'Um Mitternacht' with its passages of quiet, brooding sadness, rising to a height of almost Wagnerian power towards the end. Mahler has been a very much neglected composer in this country, who is now rapidly coming into his own. Where Germany and Holland have always liked his symphonies and his smaller works, Britain has heard very little of them. Critics have been apt to be rather condescending; either accusing him of unrelieved gloom, or else looking askance on the 'romantic' element in his work. 'A missed Wagner' has been one rather absurd verdict. Mahler himself, who died worn out and dispirited with the world in 1910, prophesied, 'My time will come,' and those words are still in process of coming true.

It was not until Kathleen met the great German conductor Bruno Walter that she was to reach the heights in Mahler. Walter himself had been Mahler's pupil and disciple, and he was the greatest living exponent of the music.

Bruno Walter had been asked to conduct Mahler's *Das Lied von der Erde* (*The Song of the Earth*) at Edinburgh that autumn for the first Edinburgh Festival. He was looking for a contralto for this enormously exacting work, which at the time of their meeting was unknown to Kathleen. After she had sung some *Lieder* for him (this took place at their first meeting, when they were introduced by Rudolf Bing at the house of Mr. and Mrs. Hamish Hamilton), he asked her to sing some lines from *The Song of the Earth*. She did so with an ease and beauty of tone that gave him the greatest pleasure —in his own words: 'I recognized with delight that here was potentially one of the greatest singers of our time.'

Their work together was to be both a joy and lasting inspiration to Kathleen. It was an honour for any singer to be chosen by Bruno Walter, and particularly in the case of this work of Mahler's. The fact that she was willing to undertake the task showed that both her confidence and her powers had increased since Glyndebourne. Although she was constantly hard at work, giving her own recitals, and taking part in performances such as *The Dream of Gerontius* at the Albert Hall and the *St. Matthew Passion* in the beautiful setting of Southwark Cathedral, she was still willing to widen her experience by continuous learning, very often in a foreign language. For *Das Lied von der Erde* she had to learn a quite considerable amount of German; and now there loomed ahead her second opera, to be sung in Italian. Because before the Edinburgh Festival in the autumn, another summer was starting with her second season at Glyndebourne, this time in Gluck's beautiful eighteenth century opera *Orfeo*.

CHAPTER

9

Now that Kathleen was famous, considerably better off after a life of hard work in which money had never been plentiful, and with new friends among people whose names were often very well known indeed, under it all she remained exactly the same. Warm-hearted, sweet-natured, and always ready to welcome friends who appeared from her old life in the North with pleasure, she was never too busy after a tiring recital to single out folk she had known in the most crowded dressing-room or pressing circle of eager fans. She had more poise now, and her charm had matured into a gracious ease of manner, but she never became in any way 'grand'. Like all truly gifted people her modesty was never assumed, for the very good reason it did not need to be. Always completely her natural self, it was no wonder that besides being tremendously admired she was also greatly loved.

But that did not mean Kathleen allowed everyone who wished to, to become her friend. There are always in the world of music or the stage, hangers-on who wish to claim gushing acquaintance with a 'name', and try to turn themselves into bosom friends, when in reality all they want is a bit of reflected glory. There are others who invite well-known singers to their private parties and then expect them to sing after a long and tiring day. Sometimes thoughtless, sometimes merely ill-mannered, such people can become perfect pests if allowed. But Kathleen had her own gentle direct way of dealing snubs where they were needed, though no one could be kinder to the genuine fan or autograph hunter.

She had a keen wit too, especially where people she did not like were concerned, and a gift of mimicry that could be used to devastating effect if she had come across someone pompous or condescending. With critics, who were sometimes needlessly severe, she was at this time often too ready to acknowledge them as right and feel that she must need improvement in whatever fault was pointed out. This was not always so, because although they would not acknowledge it, there is a certain type of critic who can quite often be wrong.

So far as friendship was concerned, Gerald Moore has said that no one could hope to be a friend of hers who was tinged in the slightest degree with meanness or deceit. And perhaps that was why she had such good friends round her in her immediate circle. Quietly modest where she herself was concerned and of true sterling worth, she seemed to attract others of the same cast. Her friends were good friends, because she her-self was good, and all true friendship is an equal give and take. A good listener, she avoided bores, and so the company around her was usually either interesting or amusing. Her strength of character made her always able to cut out the parasites and hangers-on who can so often litter a pathway to fame.

Before going back to Glyndebourne in May 1947 Kathleen took lessons in Italian, and learned her part in the opera with her usual thoroughness. So it was with only some of her former nervousness to shadow things that she once again came to the lovely old house on the Downs, to settle in for a stay of some weeks. For a while at least, there need be no more travelling by rail to all four corners of the Kingdom; no more uncertain meals or wondering whether at the end of the journey the hotel would be good, mediocre or down-right bad. She could look forward to working in beautiful surroundings with pleasant people.

Again Kathleen was singing the name part, on this occasion that of the Greek hero Orpheus, which in these days is always taken by a woman, a contralto.

Gluck was born in 1714, and was a contemporary of Mozart, though the latter was not born until 1756. But Mozart spent his brilliance early, dying in 1791 at the early age of thirty-six; while Gluck died an old man for those days in 1787. *Orfeo* was first performed in Vienna with an Italian libretto in 1762; it was then altered and recast for Paris where it was performed in French in 1764, a year which marked the end of Gluck's ten years' directorship of the Vienna Opera House. *Orfeo*, Percy Scholes notes in *The Oxford Companion To Music*, is the earliest opera of any composer still to maintain a regular place in any repertory; which is not surprising, considering the pure and classic beauty of the music.

Gluck was not the first composer by a long way to

take the famous Greek legend and turn it into an opera. Almost the first opera known in musical history is the sixteenth century composer Peri's *Eurydice* written in 1600 or just before; and there was a performance of Monteverdi's *Orpheus* given at Mantua seven years later.

Gluck's *Orfeo* is not only full of the most beautiful music, but the name-part demands a high perfection of singing that is seldom heard; perhaps not more than once in a century. Kathleen's voice seemed to have been made specially to suit Gluck's score; not only that, but she looked incomparably beautiful in the role. This is mentioned in Glyndebourne's own delightful brochure which remarks: 'Gluck's *Orfeo* was notable for the appearance of Kathleen Ferrier in a role for which Nature and Gluck, with uncanny prescience, designed her.'

From the first Kathleen took naturally to the music, and Carl Ebert's help was of infinite value to her. The American singer Anne Ayars was the beautiful Eurydice, and the Greek soprano Zoe Vlachopoulos was Amore—there were only these three singers to head the cast as the legend tells of the hero Orpheus, his wife Eurydice, and Amore the God of Love.

The original legend had a starkly tragic ending, but Gluck gave his opera a happy finale which, though it might please the less classical-minded among his audiences, was certainly very inartistic.

The Glyndebourne production was, as usual, exquisitely done with strikingly affective scenery. The opera is in four acts, the first being a Grotto with the tomb of Eurydice at which Orpheus and his friends mourn his dead wife. Amore, the God of Love, takes pity on the husband's frantic grief, and descends from

Olympus to comfort him. Orpheus is famed through this world and the one of shadows for his marvellous playing upon his lyre, and Amore tells him that he may go down to Hades, the realms of the dead, and see if he can prevail upon its guardians by his music to allow him to bring his wife out of the shadows back to the land of the living. But if success should be his, he must not look on Eurydice's face as they return, or he will lose her again, this time for ever.

The second act is 'The Abode of the Furies' where Orpheus implores the aid of the Shades. His grief and his lovely music move their pity, and they open the gates leading to the Valley of the Blest. Here, in Act Three, Eurydice and the blessed spirits sing of the celestial joys. Orpheus is welcomed, and his music prevails. Eurydice is given back to him and, not daring to look upon her face, he leads her up into the world of the living.

Act Four takes place in a lonely wood, and Eurydice, at first overcome with joy, is unable to understand why Orpheus will not look upon her, and he dare say nothing of the reason. She thinks he no longer loves her, and says wildly that without his love she would rather be dead again. Tortured by her pleading Orpheus clasps her in his arms and looks into her face. And as he does so she falls dead.

In the beautiful aria, 'Che faro', or in English:

> What is life to me without thee,
> What is left if thou art dead?
> What is life, life without thee,
> What is life without my love,
> What is life if thou art dead?

Orpheus is in the most bitter anguish. But here Amore once again appears, telling him this was only a trial of his faith. The God of Love then brings Eurydice back to life, and Orpheus has not travelled down into the Underworld for nothing.

When the opera was produced in June 1947, the audience was tremendously enthusiastic; and in spite of the fact that some of the more pernickety critics found fault here and there, the majority were favourable.

But the few croaking voices only cried out in the wilderness. Kathleen received the warmest ovation from numbers of famous people, and she was destined to give untold pleasure in many parts of the world whenever she sang either the entire role or arias from the opera. *Orfeo e Eurydice* was to become, in a special sense, unique to herself.

After the end of the Glyndebourne season Kathleen took a holiday in Devonshire with her sister. She returned to London only a few weeks before the Edinburgh Festival, and rehearsals for *Das Lied von der Erde*, on the score of which she had already done a lot of work, began in good earnest.

All though Kathleen's climb to fame, the flat in Frognal Mansions had given her a fixed domestic background in the intervals of her concert tours. Her beloved father was getting old, but he still had many interests in life, and it is obvious that his daughter's fame was a source of great joy and quiet pride to him. Kathleen had always been fond of cooking, and domesticity was the ideal relaxation from the more formal life which nowadays claimed so much of her. Not that she often had time to indulge in such things as making puddings or cakes; but when the mood took her she occasionally did so. Kathleen would never have fitted into a luxury service flat in some great soulless Mayfair block, where a poky scullery and tiny stove are all that is available other than the service restaurant below, or meals on trays brought up by servants—both of which can become so deadly dull.

So the flat, though up far too many steps and in many ways old fashioned and inconvenient, was a home and hearth—complete with cat—and when, for instance, Kathleen began to take a sudden interest in painting as a hobby and dashed into it with her usual enthusiasm, the walls were adorned with the results of her work.

But there was not much time for anything but rehearsals for the great and exacting work she was learning under Dr. Bruno Walter. Mahler widened her experience as nothing else had quite done. She respected and soon came to have great affection for the great conductor, Mahler's pupil and disciple, and the greatest living interpreter of his music. The music was tearing emotionally, and Kathleen, who had had to learn to hide her sensitiveness in earlier life, found that this strange and often disturbing work pulled at her heart, and in the last great 'Farewell', tears overcame her and made rehearsals impossible to proceed with.

Probably one reason why Mahler's works have been slow to take root in Britain is because of their strongly emotional quality—a very different emotion from that roused by the romantic music of the Italians. *Das Lied von der Erde*, the *Kindertotenlieder* and the symphonies have been called 'melancholy', 'joyless', 'despairing', even 'morbid', but none of these terms really describe all of Mahler. Although much of his own unhappiness does come into the music, he always seems to be looking to horizons far beyond this world, somewhere into a distant land of visions and dawning hope. In fact, songs such as 'Um mitternacht' have been described as 'ghostly', and that description is not far wrong. And it was Kathleen's voice, more than any other, with its own almost unearthly purity and beauty that was so wonderfully suited to Mahler's songs.

Professor Walter was not in the least disturbed by Kathleen's tears; he patted her shoulder kindly, saying, 'It's all right, my child, they all do it!' Meaning that every singer of the 'Farewell' was at first overcome by its sadness.

Peter Pears sang with Kathleen in *Das Lied*, and hour after hour the intensive rehearsals went on, until at last Professor Walter and the singers themselves knew they were nearing—not perfection, for no artist ever attains that to his or her satisfaction, but something in this case coming close to it.

Kathleen's first appearance this year in Edinburgh was at a chamber concert. She sang with the Jacques Orchestra under its founder, Dr. Reginald Jacques, one of her arias being 'Prepare thyself Zion' from Bach's Christmas Oratorio.

Edinburgh was a city *en fête* for this, their first Festival; the musical élite of many countries had gathered to listen and criticize, while thousands of other visitors thronged beflagged Prince's Street, walked up to Arthur's Seat, or explored the Old Town with its

82

fascinating ancient buildings and narrow twisting streets, or else admired the beautiful eighteenth century crescents built by the Brothers Adam.

Edinburgh, 'the Athens of the North', is like no other city in Europe, or indeed in the world. Everything that happens within its walls becomes instantly and distinctively its own. At first people were inclined to sniff and talk of the Salzburg Festival, and other European musical occasions. But comparisons are always odious, and in this case were merely silly.

Kathleen soon found out all about the wonderful hospitality of the Scots; they were delighted with her, and she with them; and after the inevitable 'first night nerves' over *Das Lied*, she thoroughly enjoyed herself.

There were two performances of *Das Lied* with the Vienna Philharmonic Orchestra on 11th and 12th September. Each was magnificent, and both pro-Mahler and anti-Mahler critics had to unite in their praise of conductor, orchestra and singers. A distinguished critic wrote in *The Times*:

The performance was enhanced by the splendid singing of Miss Kathleen Ferrier, whose voice seemed to have gained an added richness, and a power which surmounted the orchestral climaxes with ease. Her command of vocal colour to give dramatic expressiveness to the words proved fully equal to the considerable demand of the songs, and these effects were accomplished without detriment to the beautiful quality of her tone.

Although there was still a good deal of adverse

criticism of Mahler as a composer, no one could deny the superb quality of this performance. And it is perhaps from this date, more than any other, that Mahler has gained an ever stronger hold on the music-going public in Britain.

So after Glyndebourne for the second season, there came resounding triumph in Edinburgh. Now Kathleen was talked of in many parts of the world; Holland clamoured for her to return to them, Scandinavia wished to hear her, Paris and Rome were interested; and across the Atlantic curiosity was mounting. After the Edinburgh Festival it was arranged that in January of 1948 she was to sail for New York.

But there was a lot of hard work to be packed into the remaining two and a half months of 1947. Once again Kathleen sang in *Messiah*, this time at Belle Vue, Manchester, with Sir Malcolm Sargent conducting. There were the Norwich and Leeds Triennial Festivals, and Kathleen also took part in Elgar's *The Music Makers*, that mighty setting of the words of the Irish poet, Arthur O'Shaughnessy. At various recitals she sang Mahler's *Kindertotenlieder*, and many other works, both classic and modern. She recorded Brahms's Alto Rhapsody, and some of her recitals which were broadcast included charming folk-songs, some of which luckily remain with us on records. There was also a revival of *The Rape of Lucretia* which toured Newcastle, Bournemouth, Oxford and London, where for the first time Kathleen found herself singing at Covent Garden.

It was little wonder that she summed up her progress in the words, 'From Carlisle to Covent Garden in five years! Lucky Kath!'

84

For the moment, and for a little while longer, it was to go on being 'Lucky Kath'. All too short a while, alas. But at present her health was good, standing up to the strain of all this intensive work.

And on New Year's Day 1948 she sailed in the *Mauretania* for New York.

CHAPTER

10

THE voyage to New York was one of uninterrupted enjoyment for Kathleen. She and her London agent John Tillett had been seen off from Waterloo by Mrs. Tillett, Mr. and Mrs. Roy Henderson and Miss Joan Cross, and from the moment she got on the boat train life became one new excitement after another, for someone who had never travelled further abroad than Holland.

In these days, when good food is just an ordinary part of life, it is difficult to imagine what travelling on a big liner meant for ration-starved English citizens in the years immediately following the war. To be able to order a good beef-steak, fresh salmon, any amount of exotic dishes and sweets, was something to be written home about to one's friends and relations. This was not in any spirit of greed but in gleeful triumph at escaping for a brief while from the drabness of a Britain that, almost alone of European countries, seemed to go on being short of everything except what was officially termed 'good, nourishing food'.

Luckily for her, Kathleen proved to be a good sailor, and even in gales and a heavy swell, remained serene

and happy. She enjoyed all the good times a luxury liner can offer, and on arrival in New York found the great city an exciting fairyland of pleasures. She was photographed and interviewed, and among welcoming gifts at her hotel she found a beautiful flowering plant from Ruth Draper, the world famous impersonator, who was also to become her great friend.

Unfortunately, things did not go on as well as they had started. Kathleen was unused to the very hot, centrally heated rooms which all New Yorkers naturally take in their stride. Emerging from an almost tropical heat into icy cold streets in the depth of a New York winter gave her the worst cold she had ever had—and this with the first concert a few days away.

But rehearsals with Bruno Walter had to be carried on somehow, and after one day of having no voice at all, it luckily returned, and the first performance of *Das Lied* at Carnegie Hall was rapturously received by the huge audience.

The critics however, were divided; some of them could not praise Kathleen highly enough, others were decidedly damping. But Bruno Walter had no doubts about the success of her performance. The more he worked with her, the more delighted he became; and there and then he promised to give her further coaching in *Lied* himself at the earliest opportunity. This, on top of all she had learned with Roy Henderson and Hans Oppenheim, was something wonderful for her; lessons from Bruno Walter would be the highest honour a *Lieder* singer could be offered.

Yet even Bruno Walter's praise, and a glowing tribute from Leopold Stokowski, did not entirely cheer Kathleen up, though notices such as one in the *Journal American* must have helped. The critic wrote:

> Miss Ferrier has a voice to thrill to. Its warmth and purity of tone, its even scale and wide range, its sheer beauty, make it an exceptional organ. It was not her voice alone that made her performance exciting. She is a true interpreter. Part of the velvet of her voice was spun from a wealth of feeling. She *lived* through the text of her part in *The Song of the Earth*. Her singing reflected its meaning and she communicated her feelings with artless simplicity. That is the height of artistry.

This must have been somewhat comforting after the rather blighting remark from another paper that, 'The high hopes held for Kathleen Ferrier the English mezzo [*sic*] were not fulfilled.'

The next concerts were to be given in Ottawa, Illinois, and Chicago. This meant travelling to Chicago, and then catching another train for a further two hours journey to the small town with mostly wooden houses, where after many hours travelling Kathleen felt tired and very nervous.

The concert was in a school hall, which on this occasion held nearly a thousand people. The audience gave Kathleen a wildly enthusiastic reception, and were genuinely thrilled with her. This was gratifying and heart-warming, and she returned to Chicago considerably cheered up.

Next day came her concert in Chicago, and this too went off very successfully. Then she gave her big recital of the visit in the ballroom of the big hotel where she was staying (from which she had a wonderful view of Lake Michigan), and again there was success. Claudia Cassidy, the most important critic in the Middle West, wrote of Kathleen in the *Chicago Daily Tribune* in a manner that was both just and fair, and as her good opinion was to be valued, Kathleen returned to New York knowing that her Middle West début had gone off extremely well.

Back in New York Bruno Walter gave the first promised lessons in *Lieder*. She was both inspired and helped by his kindness and advice, and he promised to resume their lessons as soon as mutual engagements allowed it.

The remaining days of Kathleen's stay were filled with visits to museums, shopping and window gazing in the fabulous stores, being entertained by various friends and acquaintances. Kathleen was learning for the first time the generosity of American hospitality, that lasted up to the moment when she sailed in the *Queen Mary* for home.

The weather was rough, and the great ship docked several hours late on 10th February, 1948, leaving Kathleen only a few hours respite before taking part in *The Dream of Gerontius* at the Albert Hall the next day.

Around this time there was a newcomer to the Frognal household. Kathleen's beloved father, though still taking a lively interest in everything, was eighty years old, and it was necessary that someone should be constantly in the flat with him. Also, Kathleen's sister, who was now head of a school in Chiswick, found the housekeeping and travelling to and from her work rather too much. It was Roy Henderson who solved the problem; one of his pupils Patricia Jewett was looking for somewhere to live, and was willing to housekeep while she continued her singing studies. The arrangement worked out excellently, and 'Paddy' became one of the family and took over all the housekeeping and running of the flat, including looking after old Mr. Ferrier.

Paddy had worked in a market garden during the war, and Kathleen who always loved flowers and the country had longed for a garden of her own. There was a small, arid plot of ground behind the flats, a haunt of cats and in the shadow of a tree; but Kathleen asked the Landlord's permission and decided to try and create a garden. Helped by Paddy, Kathleen actually managed to make one on a tiny scale, buying plants and packets of seeds and even gardening books. It is often touching to see what boundless enthusiasm and faith can do in the most unpromising plots of London soil, in far less fertile parts of the city than Hampstead. Perhaps one of the worst features of huge modern blocks of flats is that so many thousands of people who once enjoyed little houses with small gardens that could be miniature miracles of flowers and fruit, now have nothing except a few formal grass plots and flower-beds surrounded by brick and concrete.

Kathleen also brought every now and then something to improve the flat. She had a love for antique furniture and glass, and a natural good taste. Also her visits to museums and art galleries, both here and in America, helped her to learn something of good painting, especially as her great friends Mr. and Mrs. Maitland's collection of pictures included such famous names as Gaugin and Van Gogh. And for the first time in her life Kathleen made time to read more, her tastes naturally inclining towards musical subjects.

Photography was also a hobby of hers, and the gift of a fine camera from her sister gave her a great deal of fun and pleasure. Roy Henderson tells of her pleasure in setting up her camera for a time exposure, and then running round to pose with himself, his wife and his father, for a charming group at the door of the waiting-room in his house. The picture shows a Kathleen happy among her friends, and is specially delightful as it shows her in what must be the only photograph of herself and her 'beloved Prof' side by side.

She was always happy when visiting friends. Gerald Moore says that laughter was never far from the surface with Kathleen. His insight and affection may be summed up in his own words: 'She loved to laugh; her life was laughter,' and one may add that she was never happier than when with him and the few, chosen friends of her inner circle. Her warmth and gaiety attracted many who liked to look on themselves as her friends. But the very special warmth and intimate sharing of similar tastes was something she kept for only a very few. A select band, joined in the last few years by Sir John Barbirolli, his wife and mother. Kathleen was always fond of elderly people—her 'Prof's' father and Sir John Barbirolli's mother were special friends; and she loved all children, being happy in their company.

In April 1948 Kathleen made her second trip to Holland, to sing there for the first time as a solo artist. Peter Diamand, the Dutch impresario, had wanted her to undertake a concert tour some time before this, but pressure of other engagements had not made it possible.

There was to be a broadcast of *Kindertotenlieder* from Hilversum, and several recitals. On this tour the bulb fields were in bloom, mile upon mile of vivid colour, like some gigantic patchwork-quilt with the silver thread of the canals running through it, and an embroidery of windmills. Again the slow smiling, friendly people, the clean neatness of the houses, the quiet beauty of old cities, all delighted Kathleen. She loved the land and the people, and they loved her in return.

The Press acclaimed her. On 12th April Bertus Van Lier wrote in *Het Parool*:

It is not surprising that the owner of this wonderful contralto voice became famous in so little time, and that Bruno Walter immediately gave her an engagement in America, after he had heard her sing in Edinburgh! For really: all that one can wish for in singing in one's dreams is here materialized; a voice like a bell, varying from velvety softness to silvery lustre, a technique so effortlessly perfect that everyone stops believing that singing is difficult; apart from the simplicity and purity of interpretation as one very seldom hears: in a word delightful.

She returned to England, only to have to travel back to Holland a week later, this time by aeroplane. She never liked aeroplanes, but pressure of time would not permit the sea journey. She took part in a performance of *Das Lied* conducted by Van Otterloo in Utrecht; and there was a recital in Amsterdam before the trip home.

Two months later found Kathleen in the Netherlands for the third time that year, taking part in the Holland Festival. There were more performances of *Das Lied* in Amsterdam and Schevenigen.

The time had come when, however little she liked flying, she could no longer avoid it. A brief holiday in Northern Ireland followed by more work in England, and she was on her way by air to Scandinavia for a concert in Copenhagen on 20th September. A few days later she was asked to sing at a Memorial Service for Count Bernadotte in the Swedish Church. Then there were three recitals, in Copenhagen, and two other Danish cities. The critics as well as the audiences went wild with enthusiasm. Kathleen's gift was one the musical Danes could appreciate without hesitation, and her triumph was complete.

Yet another visit to Holland came in January 1948. This time Kathleen took Phyllis Spurr as her accompanist. As always they both got on excellently together, and the recitals were everything that could be wished.

By now Kathleen felt completely at home in Holland. Everyone, everywhere she went could not make enough fuss of her, and it was no wonder that she was so happy in her work and her surroundings.

But February 1949 meant the beginning of her second American Tour, and on the 18th of that month she was once more boarding the *Queen Mary* at Southampton.

CHAPTER

11

THE great liner docked thirty-six hours late, and there was little time in which to rehearse for the first engagement. This was a concert performance of *Orfeo* with her lovely Eurydice of Glyndebourne days, Anne Ayars. They were both looking eagerly forward to working together again, so it was especially fortunate that this, one of Kathleen's favourite roles, was being undertaken with someone she knew and liked.

The performance was at the Town Hall, New York, and it was the commencement of a much longer tour than the first. It would range from the Eastern States, through the Middle West, across to California. Canada was to be visited, and there would be a journey down to tropical Cuba.

This meant a great many hours on interminable train journeys; but at least it gave her an opportunity to catch up on correspondence, though none could reach her for days at a time with such vast distances being covered so quickly.

Orfeo, which marked the launching of the tour, proved an instant success. New York was electrified, and this time the audience rose to her wild with enthusiasm.

Afterwards Kathleen was busy rehearsing with Arpad Sandor, who was to be her accompanist on tour. There was also time for a lesson with Bruno Walter. But let Kathleen tell the next part of the story in her own words. These extracts are from a letter to Roy Henderson, written on Canadian Pacific Railway notepaper, and headed 'Somewhere between Ottawa and Toronto' dated '31st March, '49'. She wrote:

Dearest most beloved Prof,

I have been waiting to write until my recital was over, so that I should have lots to tell you, so here goes. I expect Paddy has kept you 'primed' with snippets of news and sent you all my love on several occasions.

I'll start at the beginning with the voyage which was a riot from beginning to end and I was delighted we were nearly two days late to prolong the fun. An hour extra each day too because of going westwards— it was just heavenly!

I ping-ponged and danced and shuffleboarded and even played golf shots into a net! I was so stiff I couldn't move for two days!

Then *Orfeo* with Anne Ayars and Tommy Schermann conducting . . . with the audience going mad and the critics too. . . . Then I had a few days in New York to rehearse with pianist and see about Income Tax and other dull jobs, and had two hours with Bruno Walter re Edinburgh. He altered my programme quite a bit, and I now have 6 new Brahms to learn and 2 Schubert, but he's such a love I don't mind, except that I wish I had a chance to try them out before Edinburgh. Phew!

Here Kathleen gives a list of her amended programme, and as always asks for the seal of her 'Prof's'
approval, in this case with a gay 'Okey-doke, love?'
She then goes on to describe her concert at Granville,
Ohio:

The concert was in a church which held about
2,500 people and some of the audience never saw me
all night 'cos they were knitting! Oh my I was de-
pressed. . . .

So, we may guess, would any singer have been, but
perhaps the knitters felt they could concentrate on the
music better. What is rather surprising is that the real
music lovers in the audience did not stab them with
their own needles!
Kathleen continues:

So from there we had to catch a train at 2 a.m. for
Montreal via New York. In to N.Y. at 4 p.m. the
next day, and another night on a train (the 3rd) to
Montreal. Wakened at 7.15 a.m. by customs, and in
the hotel, looking like death mashed, at about 8.30
with an important recital at 3 in the afternoon . . .
this concert . . . was packed with ardent music lovers
—a nice room holding about 800—and they just
went mad. An official tea followed, and then dinner
with 6 of the nicest pets ever, and I was feeling a lot
better. . . .

Kathleen had a special love for the Canadians from
the first day of her setting foot on their soil; a love which

they returned with all their warmth. The next part of her tour took her back into the States:

Then off again for *another* night train, the 4th in succession for Indianapolis—via Toronto and Detroit (two nights travelling making the 5th! then another whole day to Pittsburg—only this time the train broke down 4 times and instead of arriving at 10.25 p.m. it was 2.15 A.M.!

Well, that was my first week on the road. . . . Then I had two days to recover before the Pittsburg recital and I was ready for it. . . . The concerts have all gone very well, some quite thrilling as regards audience reaction, and others ordinarily enthusiastic. But here (Canada) the halls are very well filled. Last night there were 2,500 again in Ottawa!

Then back in New York with four days off before my town hall recital. It was good to have tried the hall out in Orfeo—I felt at home there.

I had four more hours with Bruno Walter which were wonderful,

she adds, and then goes on to describe her New York concert:

I wore my new red dark satin and no jewellery whatsoever except my ring. . . . People were standing and there were 100 sitting on the stage! It hasn't happened before for years I was told. . . . I walked on, and mi pals must have been there, because the clapping went on for 5 mins before I could start. That was touching and encouraging, and I put my all into it, and the audience just shouted and stamped. It was lovely, Prof dear, and I think you'd have been happy if you'd been there. . . .

Bruno Walter and his daughter were among the distinguished audience, and Kathleen continued:

Bruno Walter rang me up the next morning to ask to be excused for not coming round, but there was such a crowd. He said some of the loveliest things I could ever have dreamed of hearing, and he said 2 or 3 times that he was very proud of me. . . .

And here Kathleen has something to say of what the critics wrote about her!

Well, the papers next day were mixed. They all criticized something. One said I could have been better gowned! One said I was breathy—another said I wasn't intense enough—another very intense— another it was a pity that, like Marian Anderson, I couldn't sing the bottom F sharp in Todd das Madchen. Of course it's D, and a 3rd lower if he had the sense to know, which makes quite a difference! But in a grudging way they said I was worth watching! . . . I think the audience are often the judges in the long run, and they were wonderful. . . .

She signs the end of her long letter, after sending love to Mrs. Henderson and everyone at home: 'Your adoring "pupe", Klever Kaff.'

Although the American press was still giving her a mixed reception, nearly everywhere she went, the audiences themselves welcomed her wholeheartedly. In April her accompanist fell ill and had to give up, but Kathleen had a stroke of luck in getting John Newmark. From that time on, no one else ever accompanied her in America. He joined her while she was in Wisconsin, and from their first rehearsal they got on well together. For the rest of the tour, he was not only her accompanist, but organized travelling agenda and concert arrangements. He took her sight-seeing whenever they reached an interesting place, saw that many of the irritating everyday worries which had beset her earlier were done away with, and altogether made life much more cheerful.

The tour continued down across the map, going from Minnesota where she gave a concert in St. Paul, the capital, to the Deep South, Georgia and Kentucky.

The next port of call was Havana, the colourful capital of Cuba, since torn by civil war, but at that time a gay and cosmopolitan city. For the first time Kathleen saw the blazing skies and brilliantly coloured flowers of the Caribbean. At midnight after the theatres were closed, the gay Cubans still strolled the boulevards, or sat outside the cafés sipping drinks and arguing politics until the small hours. A warm soft wind swept in from the sea under a sky of dark blue velvet, golden with stars and an apricot moon. The haunting throbbing music, some of it a legacy from Spain four hundred years ago, lilted through the night, and Kathleen once went off exploring by herself. The shuttered windows of tall houses in narrow streets kept their secrets safe, and there were glimpses of flower-bright patios and gardens where orchids glowed and flamed from among tropical foliage. Many of the swarthy, smiling people she passed had the blood of pirates in their veins, some of the men still looking like buccaneers of the Spanish Main. Kathleen, so Roy Henderson tells us, liked to think she was descended from Henry Morgan the notorious pirate; and here she was, very near the seas he had once sailed under the dreaded black and white flag.

This part of the tour over, she flew to Miami for a well-earned brief holiday, followed by another concert. And so back to New York, and a week later she sailed home in the *Queen Elizabeth*. Before she went, another and still more exhaustive tour was arranged for the following year; a tour that was destined to be Kathleen's last in America. But in this year of 1949, only a few days at home were in store for her, before she was once again off on a round of fresh engagements, this time in Europe.

CHAPTER

12

ALTHOUGH it was at this time that a birthday present of oil-paints from her sister set Kathleen off on her hobby of painting for fun and relaxation, she had little time in which to go on with it. Photography and golf, which she still always played whenever she could get a game had to take back seats too. On 10th June she flew to Holland for a production of *Orfeo* at the Holland Festival. There was to be a fortnight's rehearsals, and Kathleen decided to get every moment's enjoyment she could out of her stay. She invited her sister and Mr. and Mrs. Maitland over, and she took a night off to see *Manon* in Amsterdam where she and the company were staying.

The opening night of *Orfeo* was a Gala Performance before Queen Juliana and Prince Bernhard, and there followed a banquet for the opera company.

During the rest of her stay Kathleen also saw Mozart's *Il Seraglio*, which she liked, and Richard Strauss's *Der Rosenkavalier* which she did not. These visits were fitted in between her own rehearsals—not only for *Orfeo*, but for some Bach and Purcell as well as Benjamin Britten's *Spring Symphony* the world premiere of which took place on 14th July.

Back home once more, Kathleen gave a broadcast recital and sang Brahms's *Four Serious Songs* at a Promenade Concert. She had then planned to take a few weeks' holiday in Switzerland, but though she went there for ten days, her plans were altered by Bruno Walter asking her to take part once again in *Das Lied*, this time at Salzburg to which he was returning after a gap of twelve years. Kathleen was very tired and not feeling too well, but she agreed at once to do what Bruno Walter wanted. In any case, to be asked to sing at Salzburg was a great honour, apart from the invitation coming from someone with whom she loved working.

The brief holiday spent amid lovely Swiss valleys in the shadow of the Jungfrau, provided a much needed rest and a time of complete relaxation. It may have been that her extreme tiredness was a foreshadowing of her illness, though no one at this time guessed it. She had been worried about herself, and Roy Henderson had insisted on taking her to a doctor as far back as 1944. But she had been given a clear bill of health and was happy and relieved over it. Anyhow, this holiday, though not long enough, recruited some of her strained energies.

As the first English singer at the Salzburg Festival, *Das Lied* was something of a renewed ordeal. It was one thing to have sung it again and again before English-speaking audiences; quite another to venture her German in front of a German-speaking audience, who knew their Mahler in a way nobody in Britain or America could hope to. But after the first rehearsal, her confidence, gained in her delight at once more working with Bruno Walter, completely returned.

Salzburg, with its ancient castle and spires, its lovely squares and old streets, its famous hotels and cafés and its Mozarteum is one of the greatest, if not the greatest, musical shrines in the world. The fact that Mozart, at the end of his brief life, was disgracefully neglected and even allowed by Court and people to be buried in an unknown pauper's grave, has not prevented his cult being on a grand tourist scale, almost in the style of Shakespeare at Stratford on Avon. But no overcrowding or hordes of tourists can detract from the perfection of the productions at the Mozart Festival, as anyone fortunate enough to have been present can testify. In this case the performance of *Das Lied* was everything even the most exacting listener could wish for. Kathleen was an enormous success, and the *Wiener Tageblatt* stated, 'The young Kathleen Ferrier justified Professor Walter's gift for discovering singers,' and went on to praise her interpretation of Mahler. After this, all fears dissolved, Kathleen enjoyed herself for the rest of her stay, listening to music and sightseeing.

In October there was another Edinburgh Festival, with the songs suggested to her by Bruno Walter when she had been with him in America. Again the Edinburgh audiences greeted her with enthusiasm; already she seemed to have become part of the musical season in the Scottish capital.

Her next visit abroad was after Edinburgh, when she went with Phyllis Spurr on her second visit to Scandinavia. Every concert she gave in Copenhagen meant 'House Full' notices, and her broadcasts were major musical events. Audiences went wild over her, and she had to give so many encores at each concert that often the piano had to be shut and lights dimmed before everyone would at last go reluctantly home.

She learnt a Danish song in a day, being coached phonetically, and in Oslo she learnt one in Norwegian —no mean feat for a stranger to each language.

The triumphs in Scandinavia behind her, the next foreign engagement was in Paris, a recital given in the Salle Gaveau arranged by L'Association Française d'Action Artistique. The critical Parisian audience were captivated by her singing, and rose to her in great enthusiasm. *Paroles Francaises* announced : 'This English singer conquered Paris with the opening bars of her Schubert *Lieder*.' Here was yet another in the long series of enthusiastic tributes Kathleen collected in this eventful year.

By Christmas she was once more on board the *Queen Elizabeth*, on her way to her third and last American tour. Her arrival was greeted with a wonderful party given by Ruth Draper. She again had John Newmark to smooth the way for her, and this tour was the most successful of all. There was an even greater amount of travelling than formerly, and a highlight was her stay in Beverly Hills. She stayed for a time at Bruno Walter's house where, although he was not in America, his servants looked after her perfectly. Kathleen saw Sunset Boulevard, and the other sights of the fabulous film city, including the famous Hollywood Bowl, that fantastic auditorium that holds twenty thousand people. The Californians fell over each other in their enthusiasm to extend their famous hospitality and Kathleen had a wonderful stay. She also greatly enjoyed a week's visit to Anne Ayars' parents before going on to three concert performances of *Orfeo* in San Francisco. It was here that the world-famous coloured singer Marian Anderson put back her own departure a day to hear a rehearsal. She was full of praise for Kathleen, and there was a pleasurable meeting between them.

About this time Kathleen was working hard on an entirely new type of work. Sir John Barbirolli wanted her to learn Chausson's 'Poème de l'Amour et de la Mer', and although Kathleen had never sung a word of French before, she decided to attempt it. She received coaching in the language from John Newmark who got Paul Roussel, a French friend of his in Montreal to make a record of the Chausson poems. This helped Kathleen enormously, and she took the record back to England with her for further study.

It was at this time that an offer for a part in the film *The Tales of Hoffman* came through Mrs. Tillett, but Kathleen was unenthusiastic. She never appeared on the screen in the whole of her career.

Steadily the names unrolled on the vast map: Fulton, Missouri with its beautiful rolling country; Omaha, Nebraska; Los Angeles; San Francisco; and on to Montreal where the critic of the *Montreal Gazette* said with truth, 'Miss Ferrier is one of the greatest singers of the present century.' After this there was a recital in New York at Hunter College, with Bruno Walter. The end of the tour came at Toronto, 27th March, 1950. It was one of the greatest triumphs of all, and Hugh Thomson in the *Toronto Star* summed up the grand finale: 'Staid Massey Hall resounded to the roar of applause, mingled with shouting and stamping.'

Kathleen promised to return, not the next season for she would be too busy, but the one after that. A promise she was, alas, never able to fulfil, owing to the illness that was so soon to overtake her.

Returning to Europe, June found Kathleen in Vienna, taking part in the Bach Festival. At this time Vienna was still rather a depressing city, full of the soldiers of four nations, and with a great deal of poverty in evidence. Its present sparkle and return of at least a shadow of its once great gaiety was not then particularly evident, and the weather was very hot.

But Vienna was still, as always, the supreme capital of music, and the Viennese were delighted with Kathleen. There were the shops on the famous Prater, the Vienna Woods, and the beautiful Stadt park.

From Vienna she went to Zürich for a concert, and then on to Milan where she was taking part in a performance of the Bach Mass at La Scala. It was an ordeal but also a great thrill to be singing in the great Opera House, and her own performance greatly moved what is perhaps the most critical audience in the world.

Back home she was busy recording for the Decca company, and in September there was a broadcast recital of some Brahms *Lieder*, with Frederick Stone accompanying her. Then there was once again the Edinburgh Festival with Bruno Walter, and in November she set off with Gerald Moore for a tour of Holland to give a series of recitals.

Kathleen was always at her very happiest when singing with Gerald Moore. And of all the many world-famous singers he has accompanied, working with Kathleen gave Mr. Moore the greatest pleasure. He himself has written, 'With no singer did I find myself more intimately at one than when accompanying Kathleen Ferrier.'

Among other recitals on this tour they gave one of *Lieder* at the Volks University in Rotterdam. Gerald Moore has the happiest memories of Kathleen's bubbling laughter and sense of fun—and this too in days when her illness must have already been shadowing life for her. Once she walked him for miles beyond Amsterdam, insisting that she knew the way back to the hotel from where the long walk had started; when she finally had to admit they were lost in good earnest and he had better ask the way to their hotel, he retorted that it would be much better to ask the way back to Amsterdam!

At the end of the tour he wrote to her: 'Certainly I have felt happy all the time—thanks entirely to your sweet nature, your unselfishness and un-prima donnaishness!'

Kathleen did not travel abroad again during 1950, and the Christmas brought her family together under one roof for the first time in years.

When Christmas Day was over, Mr. Ferrier made the remark he always did at the end—that it was the best Christmas he had ever had.

As it happened, it was to be his last. Very soon afterwards he caught influenza and had to go to bed. Kathleen had to fly to Holland in wintry weather at the beginning of January for *Orfeo* in Amsterdam. She then had engagements in Paris and Rome; in the latter city she was not happy, and in spite of glowing notices, did not care for the audiences whose reaction she thought extremely cool.

While she was still in Rome Mr. Ferrier died; influenza at eighty-three had proved too much, and Kathleen was terribly distressed at being away from home. She wanted to abandon the tour, but her sister persuaded her that their father would not have wanted this, so Kathleen had to carry on having never, as she said herself, felt less like singing in her life. But she had to go on to Milan, broadcast from Turin, and give a recital in Perugia before going back to Paris.

A little while before Mr. Ferrier's death a new friend had come into Kathleen's life. Bernadine Hammond, who had looked after Mrs. Tillett's mother when she was ill, had been introduced to them, and both Kathleen and Paddy had taken an instant liking to her. 'Bernie' as she was known, was a Nursing Sister, but she was also a good housekeeper and could help with secretarial work. Now that Mr. Ferrier had gone, Paddy would be alone in the flat a lot, and would welcome someone else to share domesticity with. Winifred thought Mrs. Tillett's suggestion that Bernie should look after Kathleen was ideal. She and Mrs. Tillett went over to Kathleen in Paris, so that part of her sad homecoming should be broken by an advance meeting. And after this it was soon arranged that Bernie should become one of the household.

Kathleen sang Chausson's 'Poème de l'Amour et de la Mer' in Manchester that February with the Hallé Orchestra conducted by Sir John Barbirolli with whom, for the remaining years of her life, she was to sing a great deal. His friendship, and that of his wife and mother were to be of great importance to her; he and Lady Barbirolli (Evelyn Rothwell) would go round to the Hampstead flat when he was in London and play private little 'concerts' of their own: Sir John with his 'cello, his wife with the oboe and Kathleen at the piano —not the old one she had won in the childhood competition and kept so many years, but a magnificent new instrument lent her by the kindness of Dame Myra Hess.

During these last months Kathleen had been working steadfastly under growing ill health, and before she flew to Cologne in March 1951 it was arranged that she should see a doctor.

In Cologne Gerald Moore again accompanied her, and has described to the author how nervous she was about her German; but she need not have been, for the Cologne audiences gave her an ovation. But this was to be the last journey abroad for some time, for on her return, after a performance of the *St. Matthew Passion* on Good Friday, she saw the doctor who said she would have to have an immediate operation. And of course this meant no more work for the next few months.

CHAPTER

13

ONLY two weeks after the operation, her friends found Kathleen as cheerful as ever. Whatever fears she might have felt she kept to herself. Then and always she faced up to illness with an invincible courage that never faltered. Moments and days of fear she must have known, but never did she trouble even her closest friends with a complaint. She did not want to be looked on as ill, and the best contribution they could add to her bravery was to be cheerful themselves.

There was a gay birthday party that 22nd April, 1951, with a continual stream of visitors bringing gifts that included champagne. Sisters and nurses at the hospital loved her, for though all patients are looked after with equal care, the cheerful ones are naturally the most popular.

After coming out of hospital she went into Sussex for a brief holiday with Bernadine Hammond. From this time forward the New Zealand girl was to be her constant companion and nurse, and with the two of them it was a case of cheerfulness always breaking in. They enjoyed each other's company, and when Kathleen was strong enough, went for long country walks, and both did some painting. Kathleen had formed a little painting group of her close friends which they jokingly called 'The Elm Tree Road Group', for at this time Sir Winston Churchill's book *Painting for Pleasure* (which Kathleen had been given) was inspiring all sorts of people, well known and obscure, to relax at the easel. Kathleen's pictures were always signed 'K.K.' and many of them adorned the walls of her flat.

After her stay in Alfriston, Kathleen went to stay with Gerald and Enid Moore at their country house on Box Hill. Gerald Moore remembers how, when he had slipped into a shop to get some cigarettes, Kathleen mischievously drove his car a little way down the road, waiting delightedly for his reactions when he found car and guests vanished!

Kathleen had been learning some Brahms songs for the next Edinburgh Festival, but the first work in which she returned to the public was Bach's Mass in B Minor. The performance was conducted at the Royal Albert Hall by Dr. Jacques, and press and public alike gave her a great welcome, delighted to find that her voice was as beautiful as ever.

The next engagement was for several performances of *Orfeo*, again in Holland, and this time Bernie accompanied Kathleen. There was a great welcome, complete with a bouquet and newsreel cameras, and as always in the Netherlands Kathleen enjoyed herself, though the weather was very hot and tiring, and her strength was weakened.

Many engagements had had to be cancelled in this year, and now everyone was clamouring for her. But she still had to attend hospital regularly, and it was a struggle to go on with preparations for the Edinburgh Festival at which she was to give a recital with Bruno Walter and Chausson's 'Poème de l'Amour et de la Mer' with Sir John Barbirolli.

But that summer Kathleen did not have many engagements. She spent a good deal of time in the country, resting and seeing friends, and there was a delightful holiday with Sir John and Lady Barbirolli. They invited Kathleen down to Seaford in Sussex, and as usual she was very happy with them.

After the Edinburgh Festival in August, there came the opening of the rebuilt Free Trade Hall in Manchester. It was on this latter occasion that Kathleen sang 'Land of Hope and Glory' at Sir John Barbirolli's suggestion—a finale which produced the sort of overwhelming effect that great Melba occasioned in her Albert Hall concerts early in this century.

At Christmas she went out a good deal, and on New Year's Eve there was a big party at the Hamish Hamiltons, one of many gay occasions with these friends. She went to opera at Covent Garden and Sadlers Wells, and to the Old Vic, but the end of the first week in January saw her at work again. She sang Brahms's *Four Serious Songs*, in the transcription by Sir Malcolm Sargent, at a Winter Promenade Concert, and a week later came the Chausson 'Poème de l'Amour et de la Mer'. It was to have been sung with the London Symphony Orchestra under Gaston Poulet, but the wrong parts were sent over from Paris.

The result of this mix-up was that the work could not be sung with the orchestra at all. But Gerald Moore stepped into the breach, and the result for piano and

114

voice instead of with orchestral accompaniment was a brilliant performance. The *Daily Mail* said the next day:

> If we were disappointed in not being able to hear Kathleen Ferrier sing Chausson's 'Poème de l'Amour et de la Mer' with orchestral accompaniment, we had the unexpected delight of hearing Gerald Moore demonstrate how marvellous it can sound in the black and white of the piano. No wonder Miss Ferrier kissed his hand and he hers.

There followed a series of concerts, with Benjamin Britten and Peter Pears, in various parts of the country in aid of the funds of the English Opera Group, some of the programmes also being given at the Victoria and Albert Museum in London.

She flew with Gerald Moore to Belfast on 7th February, 1952, for a recital at Queen's University. It was the day after the death of King George VI, and her next engagement was taking part in the broadcast memorial concert on her return to London. In this she sang an extract from *The Dream of Gerontius*, with Sir Malcolm Sargent conducting.

After this she was not so well again for some weeks; she had to take things easily at home, reading by the fire, her cat on her knee, playing Canasta, or taking part in the little 'concerts' mentioned before, with herself at the piano and the Barbirollis with 'cello and oboe.

In March she undertook some more concerts, and there were three performances of *Das Lied* in Manchester. While she was up there the Barbirollis gave her a wonderful birthday with a lovely cake, and soon afterwards there was another thrilling event. She sang at a private party where the principal guests were Queen Elizabeth, and the Queen Mother with Princess Margaret. On this outstanding occasion Gerald Moore was at the piano.

The author heard from Gerald Moore how Kathleen, who always felt the cold intensely, and especially latterly when she was ill, was in a bad draught during her last concert at the Festival Hall. Very gracefully she went down towards a lady in the audience whose scarf was lying on her lap, and asking if she might borrow it, picked it up with one of her lovely smiles. Her request granted, she draped the scarf about her shoulders for the rest of the concert, and at the end went over and graciously returned the scarf to its delighted owner.

Both Bruno Walter and Victor Olof the head of Decca Recording Company felt that if it was in any way possible Kathleen must make a recording of *Das Lied von der Erde* in which she was now world famous. Although Kathleen was not well, she was as gallant as ever, and agreed to fly to Vienna on 13th May, 1952, where the entire work was recorded.

Soon after this, she made another record of folk songs and songs by Roger Quilter. The next highlight of this year was in July, while she and Bernie were staying with a friend in Hertfordshire. The Queen came to stay with her uncle, who lived next door, and Kathleen was asked to sing that evening.

There was a flurry to get a suitable frock from London; and after some songs, half an hour's conversation with Her Majesty. Kathleen did not know the Queen was aware she was ill; but Her Majesty was most concerned about her, though this Kathleen did not know either.

Sir John Barbirolli had long wanted Kathleen to sing *Orfeo* at Covent Garden, and during that summer it was arranged that she should do so the following year. Although she had always sung it in Italian before, this version was to be in English, so the whole part had to be re-translated and learned by heart.

Edinburgh Festival—Kathleen's last—was more of an effort than it was allowed to appear to anyone outside her own immediate circle. This time *Das Lied* was conducted by Edward Van Beinum with the Concertgebouw Orchestra from Holland. In the Festival she also sang in *The Dream of Gerontius* conducted by Barbirolli, and *Messiah*. And in October 'He was despis'd' was one of the songs she recorded with Sir Adrian Boult.

The rest of the year passed all too swiftly. A concert in Dublin with Sir John Barbirolli, where Kathleen received the honorary degree of Doctor of Music, a recital at the Royal Festival Hall in November, with a performance of *Das Lied* at the end of the same month, this time conducted by Josef Kripps. In December there was a recital up in Carlisle with Gerald Moore, and many of Kathleen's old friends attended both the recital and the big party given afterwards. Bernie, who now never left Kathleen's side, noticed she was limping rather badly. But though in pain Kathleen bravely carried on rather than disappoint the people in Carlisle.

The first of December brought an important letter

from Downing Street, but the news it contained was kept secret until at a party on New Year's Eve consisting of Kathleen, Bernie, Winifred and the Barbirolli family. Sir John turned to Kathleen, opening his speech with the words 'Dearest Commander'. Kathleen had been awarded the C.B.E. in the New Year's Honours List.

The rehearsals for *Orfeo* at Covent Garden were under the direction of Frederick Ashton, who was fully aware that Kathleen was battling bravely against illness, and had to go straight to bed and rest after she arrived home. He did everything possible to save her any undue moving about, and all through the rehearsals took endless trouble to prevent her suffering the slightest unnecessary discomfort. Kathleen was very touched by this kindness, and spoke of it often to Roy Henderson. She found it unusual to work with someone who, without a word being openly said, instinctively knew just how to help her save her failing energy, inspiring her to put forth all her strength at exactly the right time and place on the stage.

The first performance was on 3rd February, 1953, and both press and audience were as one in agreeing that Kathleen had never looked more nobly beautiful or sung so wonderfully. William Chappell, who was among the audience, has said that, 'Kathleen Ferrier looked incomparably noble. And when that first great cry of "Eurydice" sounded through the theatre it was as though a being from another world had come to life. The performance was something that can never be forgotten by anyone fortunate enough to have been present.'

All artistic London, and anyone else who could get near, packed the Opera House that night; and for the second performance the auditorium was, if anything, even more crammed.

Then half way through the second act Kathleen's leg appeared to give way; she leaned on a balustrade, continuing with her performance. Then, with the utmost beauty she sang 'Che faro'. But when the pain became too much, she leant on Eurydice's arm, and walking slowly to the wings, sat down.

The opera went on; the introduction to her last aria began, and with wonderful dignity she began to sing flawlessly. Most of the audience were unaware that something was very wrong; only her close friends knew what she suffered, and waited in agonized impatience for the curtain to come down.

It only descended for the final time after Kathleen had stood smilingly acknowledging call after call. And then she was carried to her dressing-room.

Her friends found her sitting in a chair, smiling serenely and thanking everyone for their congratulations.

But there could be no third performance; that and the intended fourth were cancelled. A few days later Kathleen was back in hospital.

Another disappointment was her being unable to go to the Investiture at Buckingham Palace on 17th February. But a C.B.E. ribbon was pinned to her pillow by Sir Benjamin Ormerod, and she was told that she would be asked to another Investiture that summer.

When, after some weeks' treatment, Kathleen was allowed out of hospital, it was plain that never again could she manage the long flights of steps at Frognal Mansions. Bernie and Winifred searched for somewhere else to live, and at last Bernie found an empty maisonette in Hamilton Terrace.

The hall led into a sitting-room looking over a fairsized garden, with a charming smaller room immediately adjoining, and there was also a bathroom on the ground floor.

Kathleen decided that it sounded the very place, and insisted on paying it a visit by ambulance. At that time it was in a state of neglect, but the possibilities could not be ignored, and it was taken. Kathleen chose wallpapers and paint, and was rather worried about her little garden at Frognal, giving instructions that her precious plants should be taken and put in the new garden.

But it was the garden that made Bernie and Winifred most worried; it was terribly neglected, and in comparison the house was easy to deal with.

And then one day they found gardeners, apparently conjured up by magic, were working busily. Ruth Draper, with exquisite thoughtfulness, had given orders for a garden to be laid out as a homecoming present for Kathleen.

At last Kathleen arrived in her new home. She loved it all, and was wonderfully happy. And as the spring decided to behave kindly for some weeks, she spent a great deal of time lying in the sun on an upholstered seat which was also a present from some more of her devoted friends.

Her birthday came, and a delightful party was given —the food and wine were a present from Sir John

Barbirolli, whose mother cooked Kathleen's favourite dishes. Kathleen had a lovely day.

But her time in her new home was all too short. In May she had to go back into hospital, and on Coronation day, that wet and blustery 2nd June, 1953, she lay between life and death.

After this for a brief while she seemed to improve; her friends hoped against hope, though Kathleen herself knew there was nothing more to be done. But still she greeted her friends, when they were able to come, with brave and comforting words.

The autumn came. And with the trees turning to burnished gold, quietly, like a falling leaf herself, Kathleen fell asleep on 8th October, and did not awake in this world.

And all the trumpets sounded for her on the other side.

What a dreadful waste! some said. And many and many of her friends, known and unknown, were shaken and desolate. The newspapers the next day carried long columns of tribute and regret. In November, Southwark Cathedral was packed with thousands from every walk of life, come to her Memorial Service.

But nothing is really wasted. It may seem so to those who are left behind, but it is not so. Especially when someone's life has been beautiful and radiant as was Kathleen Ferrier's.

We have too few records of her incomparable voice, but there is much that is lovely still to be heard. A voice that seems to come from somewhere far away, somewhere brighter and more peaceful than this earth can ever be.

Kathleen's life was a thing of loveliness. And the last words remain with one of our greatest poets. He died young too, but in these opening lines of *Endymion* John Keats brings this story to a close:

A thing of beauty is a joy for ever:
Its loveliness increases; it will never
Pass into nothingness; but still will keep
A bower quiet for us, and a sleep
Full of sweet dreams, and health, and quiet breath-
    ing.
Therefore, on every morrow, are we wreathing
A flowery band to bind us to the earth,
Spite of despondence, of the inhuman dearth
Of noble natures, of the gloomy days,
Of all the unhealthy and o'er-darkened ways,
Made for our searching: yes, in spite of all,
Some shape of beauty moves away the pall
From our dark spirits. Such the sun, the moon,
Trees old and young, sprouting a shady boon
For simple sheep; and such are daffodils
With the green world they live in; and clear rills
That for themselves a cooling covert make
'Gainst the hot season; the mid-forest brake,
Rich with a sprinkling of fair musk-rose blooms:
And such too is the grandeur of the dooms
We have imagined for the mighty dead;
All lovely tales that we have heard or read:
An endless fountain of immortal drink,
Pouring unto us from the heaven's brink.